NORTHUMBERLAND
SHADOWS OF THE PAST

NORTHUMBERLAND
SHADOWS OF THE PAST

STAN BECKENSALL

TEMPUS

Frontispiece: Gordon Highmoor's picture of a man, dog and bicycle, acknowledged.

First published 2005

Tempus Publishing Limited
The Mill, Brimscombe Port,
Stroud, Gloucestershire, GL5 2QG
www.tempus-publishing.com

British Library Cataloguing in Publication Data.
A catalogue record for this book is available from the British Library.

ISBN 0 7524 3347 4

Typesetting and origination by Tempus Publishing Limited
Printed in Great Britain

Contents

Acknowledgements

Gordon Highmoor and Birtley Aris have contributed their own special way of seeing Northumberland in their artwork, for which I am very grateful. I am delighted to be able to add more artwork by pupils from Newton Aycliffe.

Many people have read parts of the text and discussed it with me over many months as ideas took shape. I am grateful for their help and comments, but accept total responsibility for what is printed here. My thanks are due to Matthew Hutchinson and Anna Rossiter, who have been in from the beginning, and to Paul Frodsham, who read the final text and made valuable suggestions. I am grateful to Sheila White's family for allowing me to print illustration 77 and the details that accompany it.

Many adults and children have worked with me in dramatic productions over the last thirty years, and although they are too numerous to mention individually, their contribution is special too.

Almost all the photographs are my own, except those listed in the text, and I thank all those who have let me use them.

★   ★   ★

SHADOWS

Are shadows insubstantial? They can only exist when a solid object is illuminated. However, light and all other matter has mass. A shadow is still real. It is cast as a silhouette; the detail of what is contained within that outline is erased. In a sense, parts of history are like this: a general outline, lots of unanswered questions, things that we can only partially comprehend, sometimes a selection of only what we wish to believe. Even the shadow shape depends upon the angle of the light.

When we fly over a landscape or view part of it from a hilltop or slope, the angle of sunlight can throw into relief a world that has long since disappeared from our consciousness. Mounds, ditches, walls, hollow ways and minor pathways and tracks are brought to life by the shadows cast by them. Field systems, whole villages, industries and defensive enclosures are revealed to us in this way when their traces on the ground are very slight and often invisible. The time of the year and day, the time when the sun's rays are at their most oblique and low, can make all the difference between our seeing and not seeing these things. The process of illumination is not just of historical interest: the light that rakes the landscape can change colours, place different emphases on landforms and vegetation through contrasts. Cloud shadows move across the land and sea at varying speeds and varying depths of clouds boil in the skies, haloed by sunshine.

As a small boy I was led by the simplicity of lines and tune from a hymn into a world of beauty:

Now the day is over, night is drawing nigh,
Shadows of the evening steal across the sky.

Peter Pan was to lose his shadow and then part of his personality when it was trapped in a drawer; it had to be sewn on again to make him whole.

Later, the curriculum of the day brought more complex images:

Out, out brief candle!
Life's but a walking shadow; a poor player,
That struts and frets his hour upon the stage,
And then is seen no more.

Later still came the poignancy of T.S. Eliot's:

Come in under the shadow of this red rock,
And I will show you something different from either
Your shadow at morning striding behind you
Or your shadow at evening rising to meet you;
I will show you fear in a handful of dust.

Shadow-worlds and shadow-lands are those inhabited by spirits, of what is left when the body is turned to dust, or something that we can experience of another world when we are alive. They represent what we do not understand, but what we feel must be there – an afterlife, or a refusal to allow the dead to be totally forgotten, because the dead have helped to make us what we are.

These reflections offer a way of looking at Northumberland's history through both what is visible and what lies beneath.

Introduction

In *Northumberland: The Power of Place* my selection of sites came from personal involvement with them. The main premise was that some places have a powerful attraction because we may have worked hard to discover something important about them. Others are beautiful or have strong associations with past events. Others have some indefinable quality that produces an altogether different response, when perhaps the language of poetry is one way to express it.

This book concentrates on a number of themes that emerge from places, people, monuments and documents. You will be able to identify with all of them, for they are largely common parts of our experience. We are born, we die; we often share what happens between our coming in and going out, but in space and time our conditions of life vary. What we are born with, the genes that lie at our roots, will not leave us totally at the mercy of this inheritance, but will be influenced by nurture, by all the conditions of life and history that shape society. To some extent we may think ourselves free, but we are not.

Society is crucial. Unlike our Neolithic ancestors, we do not expect the bones of the dead to lie in a long mound, to be taken out periodically and circulated among our descendants, for example. Some of us, like them, may hope that in some way we will continue, even if only in short-term memory. Some hope for resurrection or an afterlife. Some believe in accountability. Shakespeare's Harry Hotspur may value reputation above all else, but the cynical Falstaff has no intention of dying for a word that is just air. *Dulce et decorum est pro patria mori*? No way, when we consider the slaughter in the great wars of our time. We change.

We may no longer accept the 'authority' of our governors, and may no longer be prepared to be dragged into conflicts for the sake of the vanities of those who in the past (and present) regarded themselves as natural rulers, for our rulers are too close to us and too exposed. Thus we see castles, great houses and beautiful furniture in a different way; all power is at someone else's expense. Where did the resources come from to make the monuments of the past? Do the fat cats deserve these things? Who suffered in the process? Do we know as much about the governed and exploited as we know about the governors? The history of battles is largely written by the victors.

Great issues of the balance of power and the balance of terror may not preoccupy us. Those who have to work all the time to earn their daily bread may not at the end of the day have much time or energy to consider issues that they feel are beyond them. We feel that we are like but unlike those around us.

To look back at history through the visible remnants of our past will not only identify us with those who have gone before, but will also emphasise how different we are from them. In a way, that is the intention of this book.

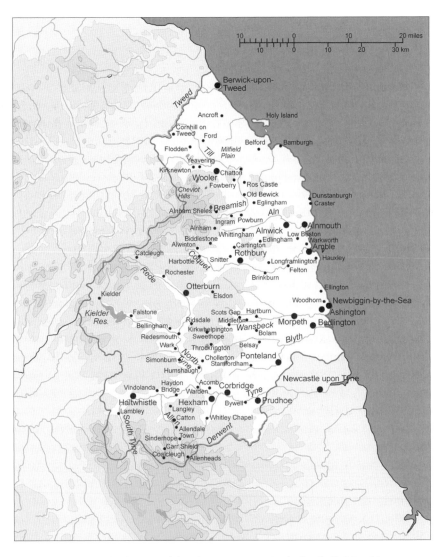

Map of Northumberland: some of the places appearing in the book. © *Marc Johnstone, Heritage Media*

one

In the beginning

Land gives us the means to live. Over time the landscape has changed because either natural forces have formed it like this or people have had some influence on it. People living in an Ice Age or in a desert have had to adapt to those cold or hot conditions; choices are always limited by our starting point. Land provides a means of survival. Sometimes its richness and our clever manipulation of it provides a surplus that, in turn, opens up a chance of leisure and development.

We are but specks of dust in a vast universe, yet we can feel that we are at its centre or even that we are controllers of our destiny. The use of the landscape into which we are born has given us the power to make choices, but the road taken always worries us with the thought of what might have been.

On the whole the places where we are born contain us, sustain us. For long periods of history it was difficult for many people to get away. A great revolution in our time transports us all over the world, or locally allows us to commute many miles from our homes. We have become more mobile, and communication has widened our minds to other places, other cultures, other times. Events are brought to us in sound and vision as they happen. Our world has become bigger and smaller at the same time. History is stored, and there has never been so much information. Paradoxically, this has not necessarily made us wiser or better. Intelligence and sensitivity are the means of sifting information to make sense of it and to decide on the next step. Forward? Backward? How should we change?

All places are the result of millions of years of change. Even those parts that we think of as 'old', such as castles, field systems or burial mounds, are minute on the earth's timescale. We may go back to the Big Bang, to the creation of the universe, but few of us can cope with the mathematics or science of that. Writers of the Old Testament coped with imponderables in a different way, by having earth created in six days with a day for the creator to rest. They placed a man at the centre of the newly created world, made woman from him, and allowed it all to go wrong; a simple, powerful story, its truth not in fact but in metaphor. It is a poem, a myth. Because we live in a created world, so it is argued, something must have created it; but how and why?

There are people who still prefer to believe this ancient story, despite the abundant scientific facts that reveal a far more complex process at work. Enquiring minds of ancient Greece noticed that there were fossilized sea creatures embedded in rock on the tops of mountains and concluded that the sea must have been there. It was an alternative to the story of Noah, which may well have been based on shared knowledge of great floods, but with a different purpose: to portray a god who punished wickedness, started life all over again and sent a rainbow as a token of a covenant between man and a pre-Christian god.

Not long ago people were thinking of the age of the earth as something like 4,000 years. Darwin's observations were feared and branded heretical because they upset the orderly stories that explained things. The 'survival of the fittest' theory was no doubt debated and rejected by many as they ate their lamb chops and kidneys and sent their children to war.

If we are to look for our past in Northumberland, we must start with the landscape formed by many complex forces: volcanoes, earthquakes, drifting continents, rises and falls in sea level, rocks deposited then ground up again, recycled, redeposited. These are forces greater than those that we have created

1 Cheviot landscape.

with our science and engineering; forces still at work, threatening climate change, floods, drought, a shift in the balance of earth's fertility.

We look below the vegetation layers, below trees, ploughed fields, grassland and water to the fundamental structure of rocks that support the cover. Geology has simplified this for the classification of rocks into igneous, metamorphic and sedimentary.

Pockets of molten rock, heated below the crust, erupted to form the core of the Cheviot Hills nearly 400 million years ago. What is left is the Cheviot itself, a core of granite surrounded by other igneous (fire-formed) rocks, mainly andesite. Today these rounded hills, cut by valleys, with a thin covering of soil farmed for centuries, are now mainly given over to grass or planted woodland. Ice sheets have taken away some of the rock and redeposited it in non-volcanic areas, often as colourful, rounded boulders. In places the bare rock is visible, particularly at such quarries as Biddlestone, where it is deep pink against the grass. Rocks have gas bubbles filled with minerals. These fire-formed hills are the highest in the county, and span the border with Scotland. (Colour 1)

Other later fire-formed rocks have pushed their way through sedimentary layers in a series of pockets – 'sills' – that are linked together. They help to form the distinct landscape, for example, of the central section of Hadrian's Wall, are a base for Bamburgh and Dunstanburgh castles, and emerge from the sea as the Farne Islands, where their vertical columns provide an ideal nesting place for sea birds. The compact, close grain provides hard stone quarries at places like Barrasford and Belford. Its technical name is quartz-dolerite, but the gorse or 'whin' that often grows on it has given it the name whinstone. Its colour varies from black to green, and when it appears in buildings, such as those at Craster, it is sombre.

Whinstone intruded into already formed rocks. The central section of Hadrian's Wall is a good place to view it in relation to other rocks. Running roughly from east to west, it is in part masked by deposits from the Ice Ages: sands, gravels and boulder clay (glacial 'till'). In the central section, the one favoured by visitors and photographers, it is exposed as bedrock, on which the wall was largely built. The scarps that are so prominent are formed by this and by 'carboniferous' rocks; limestone, mudstone, sandstone and coal. All of these rocks we see exposed in quarries, and there are limekilns that mark the seams of limestone. These rocks vary in hardness and weather differently, which adds to the variety of scenery. The whin is much tougher than its enclosing sediments, which dip south because the Cheviots were lifted up and made a dome of the sediments around the igneous centre. Ice moved in from east to west, parallel to the already established beds of rock, and emphasised the attractive scarps and dips that we see today. The availability of local stone determined how the wall was to be built. To the west, turf and timber were the building materials first used, later to be replaced by stone carried from a distance.

The rocks into which the dolerite intruded became baked when they contacted the molten rock and were 'metamorphosed' – changed. Thus sandstone became

2 Whinstone outcrop, Hadrian's Wall area.

quartzite, mudstones became whetstones and limestone produced new minerals such as garnet. At one place (Milecastle 30) the military way was paved with whetstone.

The most widespread rocks are sedimentary; formed, as the name says, by sediments laid down by thousands of years of flooding, when sands recycled from other rocks, clay and the remains of plants, animals and sea creatures form the sandstones, limestones, shales and coal seams that we see today. Much of it has been covered up by ice and later waterborne materials that give us the soils for agriculture, but the deposits lie hundreds of metres thick below this.

Of these sediments, the fell sandstones are particularly outstanding, forming scarps that lie between the Cheviot Hills and the North Sea, running from north to south, then swinging south-west through the line of the road from Alnwick to Rothbury, and onward to the west. Ros Castle and the Simonside Hills rise impressively, seen for miles around. Sandstone is the rock favoured for building, some of it beautifully compacted ('freestone'), but some of it gritty. Left in situ, where it has been twisted and tilted by earth movements, it forms little valleys flanked by rock overhangs at Shaftoe Crag, small magical places of stillness and great beauty. The bedding planes are layered, they cross one another, are full of holes in places, and erosion works on the softer parts to create shapes that artists try to capture. Holy Island Priory (Colour 2) and the southern towers of Dunstanburgh Castle, with their colourful, eroded sandstones, contrast with the more enduring and compact sandstone of Belsay Castle and Hall. The nearer to the coast, the greater the erosion.

3 *Right* Limestone pavement south of Bamburgh.

4 *Below* Howick sandstone.

5 Dunstanburgh Castle: eroded sandstone in the gateway.

The scarps became important to people of the past as drove-ways and hunting areas above the valleys, their thin soils encouraging light woodland, scrub and pasture. They have been exploited as quarries, and some of our historic past has been removed with the stone.

Throughout the sedimentary rocks are seams of coal that have been exploited for centuries locally, but the richest deposits to the south-east were the basis of the Industrial Revolution. That marked a great shift in population and its density, so that many natural features of landscape are covered over.

The past is deeply rooted in geology, and dependent on it. The rocks themselves bear traces of another kind of history: fossils.

SHADOWS OF LIFE: THE FOSSIL RECORD OF THE LONG-DEAD

> Voices in slow dying ashes spoke a whispered history
> Of swamps that fostered forest life
> Or blended in one burial leaves and fallen trees
> With brittle bones of long-dead creatures –
> Things that swam, and crept, or walked and ran.

6 Fossil tree bark in sandstone at Howick.

The earliest records of life on earth are in fossils. It is another aspect of the recycling power of nature, which captures living and dead organisms and transforms them, not into something completely different, but into a moulded copy of the original. Some forms suffer a sea change when they die there, to form part of the next series of rocks. Those with shells or bones that are made of calcium carbonate, for example, die, and as they decay the form of their remains is filled with minerals that replicate the original. The organisms are not turned to stone, but the cavities left by their structures become moulded rock forms.

Marcus Aurelius (AD 121-181), Roman Emperor, saw change in this way:

> Observe always that everything is the result of change, and get used to thinking that there is nothing Nature loves so well as to change existing forms and to make new ones like them.

'Fossils' originally meant something dug out of the earth; later it meant the remains of plants and animals found embedded in the earth's strata. The main sources of such remains in Northumberland are the sedimentary rocks. Coal measures are part of the series; it is in the mines that we find some of the most spectacularly preserved impressions of life forms, from mussels and oysters to the bark and leaves of fernlike plants. Some of the more dramatic end up in museums. One does not have to burrow deep into the earth, however, to find these shadows of the past; a walk along the fine beaches will reveal them, for example, in limestone pavements, sea coal or pebbles.

A common fossil is lithostrotion, stems of coral that mass together in cross section in small white circles, while their stems are segmented in section at the sides. More widely known and sought after are Cuthbert's beads, named after the saint, and commonly found on Holy Island's beaches. These too are coral stems that are built like a series of discs in a column. When they are detached they form flat beads that are sometimes made into necklaces. Other fossils are brachiopods, gastropods (snail-like), bivalves (like cockles and mussels), crinoids (sea lilies or feather stars) and sponges. We have a delightful specialised vocabulary here.

7 Two fossils found on the banks of the river Tweed.

8 Lithostrotion.
Hancock Museum, Tyne and Wear Museums

Rocks not only produce 'scenery', for they are a source of minerals that we have exploited and some of which we continue to exploit. Mines producing minerals such as galena for lead at places like Settlingstones and Acomb have closed, and so too have the quarries that fed limekilns almost everywhere. We are left with some opencast coalmines, quarries for igneous rock such as that at Harden Quarry, Biddlestone and whinstone quarries for road stone.

Stones in structures help to keep people in or out; Hadrian's Wall, castles, towers, houses and field walls give the landscape its character and reflect its history. Deposits of boulder clay brought down by ice provide good arable soils; the scatter of ice-strewn boulders is cleared away into cairns and walls in a slight rearrangement of this landscape. Sands and gravels have been brought down by ice or by the erosion of the Cheviot Hills by primitive farming. Commercial exploitation of sand and gravel on the Milfield Plain and at Powburn continues. Clays are used to make tiles and bricks. Lime has always been of great service to sweeten the land, to provide whitewash and disinfectant. Beneath this exploited surface lie forms of extinct life, which once dominated the landscape. All is flux: all is change.

There are many ways of seeing large sweeps of landscape, and in them trace our histories. High points such as Simonside, the Cheviot and the scarp along which the road from Alnwick to Edlingham runs are but three of many vantage points. Another way to view the whole landscape is to fly above it.

9 Powburn east quarries from the air.

10 Enclosures and fields of many periods west of Ingram, Cheviots.

Particularly revealing is oblique light, when the sun is low in the sky, for the deep shadows throw into relief features that might otherwise go unheeded. All landscapes are superficially the creation of generations of people: Towns, motorways, industries and quarries are but a few features that do not need such subtle lighting to bring them out, but the further back we go in time, the fainter are some of the traces. Aerial photography, conducted systematically, has revealed that Northumberland has one of the most intact and widespread prehistoric and medieval landscapes in Britain. There are so many because about 80 per cent of the land is pasture and moorland, and modern farming has not eliminated them. Even on intensively farmed areas, parch and crop marks in the right conditions, such as drought or as a result of a particular crop, can reveal traces of settlements. Ditches are particularly visible, even when buried, and earthworks spring out in oblique sunlight. Although in general existing surveys have revealed such sites as Romano-British farms, hill forts, bastle houses etc., it has been the more intensive approach of the past few years that has given us a more detailed view of what is still there.

Among the many new discoveries is the identification of a system of farming known as 'cord rig', known only in the last twenty years. Like corduroy, it is a series of ridges about 1m wide and shallow ditches, perhaps dug by hand. In a recent Northumberland National Park survey, ninety separate locations have been found from the air, some confirmed by excavation. All this occurs in what appeared to be an 'empty' landscape. Add to this terraces, lynchets and wide rigs and furrows that make it look as though whole areas have been combed, especially the hillsides of the Cheviots, and there is for all to see an intensively ploughed landscape now largely abandoned. The shadows of these fields and the settlements that go with them have revolutionized our knowledge of prehistoric and later communities without the need for excavation, initially. What is uppermost may cover layers of earlier occupation, the latter sometimes ignored by earlier archaeologists. We are enabled to look down, take photographs and see when walls and other boundaries overlap, and from this get a sense of change, of re-use.

From these photographs, visits to the places on the ground and careful recording using satellite technology and by excavation – either wholesale or sampling – other scientific developments such as pollen analysis and radio carbon dating fill in finer details of what was growing there, when, and how it all changed. It is a history from observation, recording and excavation without, in the case of prehistory, any documentation. It is the only way we can know what happened in the past. One result is that we know that long before the Romans came, there was settled agriculture, especially in the favoured fertile regions such as river valleys.

Such valuable research tools are not confined to ancient landscapes, but to all kinds of industrial and domestic landscapes. Flying above the earth in this way, or by looking at other people's air photographs, gives a new sense of the past. Each year new things are spotted, so that the resource has not been exhausted.

One does not have to be quite so high as in an aeroplane to appreciate what survives of the past in this way. So much history can be seen from high places. Take an example high above Rothbury to the north-west, where the edge of the sandstone scarp is echoed by the path of a carriageway built by Lord Armstrong in the nineteenth century as a feature of the park that became the setting for his house at Cragside. The immediate surroundings of that house were landscaped with lakes, which also served as reservoirs for hydraulic power, and for thousands of planted trees, bushes, small plants, footpaths and narrow roads. At the time it was reported in the press that he had turned a barren moor into fairyland. To the north-west of the house and its planted grounds he built a carriageway through and around moorland that was left pretty much to its own devices, a 'natural' environment. Today the carriageway is an access to the moor for walkers, farmers and forestry workers, its surface made of fine Harbottle granite.

To the south and west are some of the finest views of the Coquet Valley. The photograph, taken in January 2004 from above 'Old Rothbury' has much to say about the past; snow and shadows pick out three curving ramparts and ditches of an Iron Age enclosure that is possibly 2,500 years old, like so many others in the county (Colour 2). This enclosure is rather unusual in that it does not lie at the highest point in the land, but fits snugly in a sheltered valley. Beyond it

11 Cartington carriageway to the Simonside Hills over an Iron Age enclosure and the river Coquet.

the river bank rises towards the outline of Simonside on the horizon – from so many places seen as a dominant natural landmark. The enclosure may well have been the focus for a group of farmers, pastoralists and hunters seeking a living amid rich woodland, fertile soils and a river that offered fish and communication inland and towards the sea. Not far away, at West Hills, is another hill fort, its ramparts wrapped around the top of a small hill that has outcrop sandstone on which early Bronze Age cairns and rock carvings have been set.

As if to enforce the continuity of the tradition of rock-carving, someone in more recent times has carved out a strange face on the same rock as the motifs and cairn on top of it. Other signs of human interest in the area include two massive mounted millstones, lying broken against a wall and hedge. In this part of Northumberland there is much visible history, blending in with today's landscape in such a way that it could go unnoticed.

From the place where the photograph was taken you will see the whitened edge of the scarp. Other features, such as quarries, more hill forts, disused track ways, a golf course, an old racetrack and field systems are gradually revealed. Away from this edge is a landscape primarily of rock, heather and planted coniferous forest, but it is not uniform. A ditch and wall cut across it, joining carriageway to scarp edge. There are small mounds of stone irregularly placed on a plain, mostly with the core gouged out. These are probably 4,000-year-old burial cairns plundered by treasure-hunters years ago.

12 A face carved on sandstone at West Hills, Rothbury.

13 West Hills: abandoned millstones.

14 A ditch west of the Cartington carriageway.

Not far away is a giant example high above the moor, the so-called Football Cairn, with its two massive cists thrown open and scattered. It is built on outcrop that has prehistoric motifs picked into it.

The small cairns are more characteristic of the hundreds that have survived in Northumberland, and three marked rocks in their vicinity are unspectacular but significant when they are seen within the bigger picture.

Further north along the carriageway, where the land drops steeply, are rock outcrops, one of which could well have acted as a rock shelter. There is a larger one in the forest to the east, now completely grown over, on the floor of which prehistoric flints were found.

Follow the carriageway north, leave it for a while to go down towards Chirnells, and there is another unobtrusive site of prehistoric rock art in the form of a rounded boulder lying low down beside a stream.

Back on the carriageway, the vista opens up to the Cheviot Hills, with white Cheviot itself smoking with cloud, a blue sky around. Seawards the cloud is building up; more snow is on its way. Cartington Castle shines brightly below, one of the few buildings in the area (Colour 3).

Snow is a reminder of the origin of the name Snitter; it may be from Middle English 'sniteren', meaning 'to snow', and the dialect 'snitter' is a biting blast.

15 Football Cairn: a disturbed cist in a burial mound.

16 Chirnells: a cup-marked boulder.

17 Fowberry, near Wooler: cup and ring marks on an outcrop.

The landscape today reveals a new interest: people with money want to live here; new houses, many of them expensive, and with 'the benefit of central heating', are sited high up, in contrast to the past when people wanted to be out of the way of the winds. All the signs in the deep past point to hunting, farming, pastoralism, defence, death and burial. The Coquet Valley was flanked by Iron Age enclosures in unusually high numbers, mostly in high places. Rises in the land were sometimes occupied by settlements, and walls of various kinds proclaim that 'this is ours, so keep out!' Shadows of trails, many narrow and deeply rutted, link innumerable small quarries with their markets.

There are many places in the county where it is possible to look over miles of landscape like this. Signs of past lives exist either by accident or because no one wants to develop such places further. What we see are survivals that enable us to fit pieces together to make a more general picture. In prehistory, signs of life may be as minute as small pieces of flint and chert or fragments of pottery disturbed by ploughing or by burrowing animals. The density of such finds indicates possible camp sites or settlements. Burial mounds provide some of the most common survivals. The enclosure of land for farming and building speaks of life being lived; there are sufficient sites known, some of them dug or scientifically excavated to help us to understand what went on there. Many sites have been ploughed but, if the ploughing has not been too deep, ditches remain underground and show up as crop and parch marks. So do post holes and wall foundations. What we see at Cartington is on the surface, casting shadows from small bumps in the ground, lines or depressions. From the air or from hillsides, what remains after clearance and ploughing may still be seen.

Immediate pre-Roman and Roman remains are perhaps the best-known survivals; these can be either upstanding, no matter how slight, or buried. Spotting them and recording such features is exciting, and our knowledge is built up in layers, literally and metaphorically.

This is but a glimpse of histories that have been built up first of all by simply looking and by following shadowy leads, through academic disciplines, to a much more detailed picture. Information may become sparse the further back we go in time. Understanding the landscape is a prelude to understanding its history, but it is what is written down that puts flesh on bones. The narrative now moves on to more detailed sources, beginning with, paradoxically, the end of life.

two

Our going out and our coming in

The visible commemoration of death is widespread in our churchyards, traditionally 'God's Acre', and on our war memorials. Even in our short lives, fashions have changed. As a boy in an industrial working-class area I remember that if anyone in the street died, all the curtains of all the houses were closed as a mark of respect and solidarity. The viewing of the corpse was part of the ritual of death and burial. I was led to the tiny front room (used rarely, except for special occasions) to see my grandmother lying in her coffin, her face made beautiful by the undertaker. There were set phrases such as 'she looks so peaceful' and 'she looks lovely', followed by praise. There was sherry. After the funeral there was high tea with ham. The body in the coffin was lowered into the cold slit of the earth, with thuds of earth sounding like drumbeats on the lid. The sensitive mourners were left to contemplate the idea of worms destroying the body.

That was a close, personal experience. As children we experienced death too on a great scale: a pit disaster filled our church with mourners who contemplated the suffocation of men and broken bodies lying underground. The Second World War brought the telegram with the news that my pilot brother had been killed over Burma, with the letter that followed telling lies about how his body had been buried – when there was nothing left to bury. Humankind cannot bear very much reality, and the authorities were being kind.

People continue to be buried in cemeteries, seldom in church graveyards, but the dominant form now is cremation – hygienic and very much more efficient.

Northumberland has many country churchyards, where there has been a resistance to moving all the graves to the edge of the churchyard to make it easier to cut the grass and keep the graves tidy. We have a variety of shapes, sizes, materials, lettering, periods, sentiments and degrees of artistic skill. All tell us a

18 St John Lee churchyard.

great deal about society. All represent the culmination of a person's life, a possible hope for another world, and a belief that those who bury them are doing the right thing. (Colour 4)

St John Lee church, Acomb, north across the river from Hexham, is a relatively new building on an old site high above the river Tyne, detached from the village. We enter the churchyard through a lych gate, a kind of porch named after the corpse (OE: *lich*) where the service for the dead traditionally began. Seats occupy the place where the corpse used to rest. Gravestones are spread throughout the yard, some in rows, some scattered, and around the south wall of the church are early graves that were disturbed by restoration, now leaning against the wall. Among them is a huge slab that would have done justice to some important lord or cleric. Beneath the east window is a re-erected 1792 sandstone slab that has an open book, an angel's head and wings like a collar, an hourglass and a serpent swallowing its own tail. Here then are four potent symbols representing either a Bible or the book that records your life, heaven, your time running out and eternity. This group of symbols is shared at Stamfordham, with the addition of drapes, skull, angel face and scythe, on Ellen Scott's grave (1809).

By the south chancel wall is a grave arranged like a bed, made by R.B. Aves of Hexham for the burial of Henry Stubbs in 1892; William Stubbs' name has

19 Stamfordham: Ellen Scott, 1809.

been added as recently as April 2000. Look at the others and you will come across many additional family names, not all buried there, however. Very young children lie in the same graveyard as people who reached their nineties. There is an implicit sadness in the death of young children especially.

The cause of death is sometimes explicit. This was an area that mined coal, galena and witherite: in the early eighteenth century Cuthbert Todd was from the Fallowfield leade (*sic*) Mills. In 1905 William Cowing, aged nineteen, of Acomb was accidentally killed at the Fallowfield Mines. Amos Dent of Hexham 'met with an accident at Hexham Railway station' and died in 1867, aged forty-two. His infant daughter had died two years earlier; his wife died in 1884, aged sixty.

We accept that these churchyards were for everyone; 'HUBERT HORATIO SHIRLEY MORANT, BRIG GENERAL DSO 1870' shares the same graveyard, his memorial is a little more elaborate, yet many others have been seen off in some style.

Even such a brief glimpse of graves beneath the yew trees tells us much about the age in which these people lived and a little about them. The dead are also there to warn the living of what is to come. Robert Dixon died in May 1761, aged thirty-two. The mason has provided a caution:

Confide not reader in thy youth or strength
But more than both thy present moment prize
Graves here surround the (word missing)
Of each breadth and length
And thou mayst be perhaps
The next that die

This graveyard has burials that go back about 300 years. In many ways it is typical of what we find in so many others. There is a tendency for buried bones to rise to the surface when burrowing animals disturb them, for churchyards became so crowded that bodies were buried in very shallow graves, often at the expense of earlier burials. The problem of there being no room is partly solved today by the establishment of graveyards not attached to churches, and by the increasing use of cremation. It is still possible to be buried in a churchyard, but it is not a right.

What we see today is quite recent, for 300 years is not much of our history. Not everyone was buried in churchyards; criminals and excommunicates for example may have been barred. Other denominations had their own places of burial. Monks had their own set-aside places. People of power in Church and State chose to be close to the altar, or at least in the church building itself. The presence of a saint's relics attracted the hope of shared sanctity. If the saint's bones were removed to somewhere else ('translated'), the place lost its kudos.

20 Robert Dixon's headstone, 1761.

Churchyards have not remained the same over long periods of time; plague, for example, reduced the population to such an extent in the fourteenth century that there was need for more space, but once it had eased off, the population had shrunk so much that not so much space was needed. Sudden demand for more room meant that the dead were disturbed, and one wonders how people took this. If they believed in the resurrection of the actual body and parts of it were missing, what then? Was the soul more important? If so, helping it through purgatory may have been more of a concern than the fate of the body. When we die what do we take with us? People may have regarded pre-Christian practices of burying grave goods with some of the dead as wrong, but was this any worse or better than the ostentatious display of wealth that literally rose to the surface with elaborate monuments above the Christian dead? We are told that we come naked into the world and depart in the same way; we are told that it's no use laying up treasure on earth where moth and dust corrupt it, as we can't take it with us. The lesson was clearly lost on some. Even if we set aside for a moment the furniture of burial, the place was important to many, as we have glimpsed. The Northumbrian king Edwin, of Bamburgh and Yeavering fame, according to Bede had his head taken to York for burial. The rest of him was buried at Whitby. St Wilfrid (more about him later) was buried in his crypt at Ripon, but when the Scandinavians raided and later settled the north, his body was sent to Canterbury.

When Oswald was killed at Oswestry, his hands and feet were cut off and placed on stakes in 642 by Penda, who then swept through Northumbria and burnt Yeavering and Bamburgh. King Oswy was driven into Scotland, taking Cuthbert with him, but he gathered an army and returned to recover his brother's remains. He found Oswald's head and right arm (remarkably preserved and incorruptible, as Aidan had prophesied). The head was taken to Lindisfarne, his arms and hands to Bamburgh and housed in a church built for them by Oswy. Later, the head was placed in Cuthbert's coffin. St Cuthbert's body was removed from Lindisfarne, accompanied by Oswald's head, and travelled around for years before it reached Chester-le-Street. It is now in Durham Cathedral. Paintings on a fifteenth-century wooden screen in Hexham Abbey show the saint holding the king's head. Oswald's arm was stolen from Bamburgh by monks from Peterborough, and the naming of many churches after him illustrates the value of his name and relics.

It is possible, and true in some excavated cases, that new churches and other buildings were built on the sites of graveyards, some of which may not have had a church. The Norman castle at Newcastle was built on such a graveyard.

In order to see how complex the siting of burial areas was, let us take Hexham. Here Wilfrid was supposed to have established three churches. One was built above the crypt made of recycled Roman stone that we can visit today. Another smaller church lay almost touching, to the east, which became joined to the main building. A third, in response to a vow that Wilfrid made when he was in

21 Hexham: A severed head
on a fifteenth-century screen.

danger of dying abroad, may now be under the medieval church to the south of
the marketplace, swallowed up by more recent buildings. When the nave of the
priory was destroyed at the end of the thirteenth century, its rebuilding was not
achieved until the twentieth century. Until then it was used for burial of local
townspeople as an addition to the area to the north.

We know that the abbey church of today has the canons' cemetery to the
south and the town cemetery to the north, but why was an elderly lady found in
a stone cist in the latter close to the south chancel wall? Could the answer be that
she was of high status and that the place was sanctified by the holy men buried
there for centuries? Did the church facing the marketplace (the latter always an
open space) have its own cemetery for the townspeople? That we don't know
because it has been built over. We have a graphic account in the mid-nineteenth
century of the appalling state of the abbey churchyard in a public health report,
but it took years for the new Hexham cemetery to be established to the west
of the town, well away from it. Bones lay everywhere and inevitably have been

disturbed as the function of the town's churches and churchyards has changed. Some were shown little respect in the nineteenth century when the east end of the abbey was rebuilt and Beaumont Street driven through the canons' cemetery. More recent developments have been accompanied by more respect; we reburied bones in the north transept that had been disturbed when flagstones were laid around the abbey (Beckensall, 2001).

The greatest certainty in our lives is that one day we shall die. How people dispose of the dead is a profound reflection on society; it is linked to necessity, to hygiene, to status, to how much we value their lives and to the question of whether death is one big fullstop. When life is running more or less smoothly there may be time to consider what to do with the dead, whether to follow time-honoured customs. A catastrophic event, such as plague, that shakes people out of routine and custom, may call for a different approach.

We may enter our local graveyards and reflect on the meaning of words on gravestones or on their design and the materials of which they are made. Mostly they are from the early eighteenth century onwards; there are other periods in which it is impossible to find such evidence of burial; we rely on written records to know how people died and where and when they were buried. In cemeteries and graveyards symbols speak to us; a skull and crossbones, an hourglass, an open

22 Skull and crossbones, Hartburn.

book, the coiled serpent with its tail in its mouth remind us of our mortality, of time passing, of accountability to God, of eternity. The Grim Reaper, the Dance of Death point to equality in death contradicted by the aspirations of those who feel that their status in life continues beyond the grave. The early antiquarians based much of their knowledge of the deep past on what they found in burials. We use this information, but now have a more balanced view of the total environment in which people lived.

The church and its yard were a communal focus. Memorials within that church or outside it tell us something about society, about attitudes to death and about those who have died. They have much to say about decoration and taste. Access to the church was through a lych gate. The 1549 Prayer Book says that it was needed for meeting the corpse at the church, and this is where the service began. The tenth century saw the actual enclosure of churchyards. The south side was where people were originally buried. The feudal system determined the hierarchy, including who was to be buried and where. From the twelfth century onwards the rich and famous would be buried inside the church; the poor lay outside in unmarked graves, often on the north side. As there were more of them, and their graves were shallow; the level of ground rose more there, even to the top of the church wall. Bones were displaced when new graves were dug. Alas,

23 Warden lych gate.

poor Yorick appears during the digging of a grave to make way for Ophelia. Churchyards would expand and shrink according to demand. Inside the church the number of burials could became excessive and unpleasant. Important people wanted to be buried close to the altar. If there were saints' bones or other relics, this added sanctity to the church and attracted pilgrims and those who hoped for miracles. Death may have been depicted as a leveller, but some took no notice of the message and were determined to display their earthly power.

The churchyards would change size and frequency of use according to the death rate. During the Black Death of 1348-9 and subsequent plagues, when about 45 per cent of our population was carried off, the numbers of dead increased dramatically and those left to bury them diminished. Fear of infection led to a break in custom. Rich and poor alike were struck down, but there would have been few clergy to carry out the office. Where whole communities were reduced, the survivors benefited in that their labour became more valuable, and some became prosperous, changing the balance of society. They too could demand higher-status graves.

Most of the story of these changes cannot be told merely by studying churches and churchyards. We learn from written sources that churchyards had many functions: markets could be held there, especially on feast days, and dramas were enacted once they became too much in scale and content for performance in church. Sports and archery were common there, and the porches took on a social function.

What, then, of the doctrine that lay behind the graves?

Our evidence for burial in pre-Reformation times comes from archaeology, monuments, paintings, sculpture and documents. The disposal of the dead must be seen in a religious framework. Pre-Christian burial placed grave goods within the burial, although not universally; this could imply some sort of belief in an afterlife where such things might be of use. Or they could be purely symbolic of life on earth, a gesture of affection by those seeing them off. If people believed in a 'resurrection', could burnt bodies or incomplete ones reappear whole? In the Christian tradition grave goods were generally frowned upon because we can't take things with us. However, saints might be buried with rich goods; St Cuthbert is a good example. Cremation remained for centuries unacceptable.

The vivid painted interiors of medieval churches, with their scenes from the Bible, the life of saints and the Judgement, acted like a visual theological aid. People who could not read or write could view these as they stood listening to the Latin, and the messages were very clear. Hexham Abbey has a remarkable survival of paintings, not on walls, but on wood. The Dance of Death is an outstanding and rare example.

There is stone sculpture too. The table tomb in the north transept has an incised 'tree of life' under an arch, a cross from which vine leaves spring, the base of which comes from the mouths of two grotesque heads, male and female (with echoes of the pagan 'Green Man', seen also on the misericords). Like so much

24 The Dance of Death: painted in Hexham Abbey in the fifteenth century.

else in the abbey, some of the stone and wood sculptures seem ill at ease with angels, lilies and beautiful people.

It is now time to take some widespread views of church memorials in the county, examples that are repeated in many different places.

> I meet these insubstantial dwellers of the past,
> Shadows which hover over graves that bear their names
> Which intermittent sunlight throws into relief.
> Testament of life lived long ago in joy or grief and all that lies between
> Ending with hope of resurrection, hope of bliss to come.

25 Falstone: the work of a local mason.

Here is a microcosm of all history;
Recorded accidents, death of babies, proud longevity.
Each stone quarried from a living rock,
Some words that hide a depth of suffering or pride.
They stand as silent sentinels, but some have toppled into grass,
Wear coverings of moss below a canopy of branches
Or thick darkness of some ancient yew.
A serpent swallowing its tail – a symbol of eternity.
A fading hour-glass holds no sand
Yet still proclaims our time is running out.
A book of life lies open at the page that we would wish most to forget.
Skull grins above a necklace of crossed bones, stripping people to the core.
Urns and frilly curtains are more comfortable reassurances,
Words woven into verse keep loss at bay
We do not die, but pass away.
A shouldered scythe has cut the harvest of our souls.
Stone angels wait where Godhead sits in judgement on his throne.

Through a wide range, chronologically and stylistically, of churchyard and church memorials, we are brought very close to local people. One of the most poignant memorials is at Bolam: just to the left of the gate leading to the Anglo-Saxon tower of this very fine church is a headstone:

> 'Erected by Lord Decies, in memory of John and Margaret Charlton, for upwards of sixty
> years, the faithful, and respected servants, of the Bolam family
> John Charlton, died, aged 83 years
> Margaret, his wife died, aged 84 years.
> William, their son died, aged 20 years
> Margaret, their daughter died, aged 9 years
> Sabella, their daughter died, aged 6 years
> Henry, their son died, aged 14 years'.

We can only guess the pain of experiencing the death of four children. It is more personal because this happened to my parents, five of whose seven children died before they did. Bare facts are simply carved in stone.

In the same churchyard are two flat sandstone slabs with blunt lettering made, presumably, by the local mason, who reports the burial places of Thomas Robson in 1695 and John Walton in 1703.

The 'N' is reversed, words are unspaced, and letters missing first time round have been inserted. The Roman alphabet was used universally for the earliest type of lettering: strong, crude and vigorous. Fashions changed; the eighteenth century saw the effects of penmanship and a coming of contrasting styles; by the next century it is not uncommon to see many styles on the same headstone.

26 Tom Robson.

27 Joseph Walton: Bolam. A German pilot jettisoned his bombs here, and was forgiven during his visit in 2004.

There is also a uniform choice of images and designs as well as signs of individual, skilled masons at work. Local stone predominates still until more recent times, with the local masons knowing where to quarry the best. Often the choice was not very happy, so that some inscriptions were partially or completely defaced by erosion.

Many of the churchyards that house these memorials are situated on high places. Newbiggin is on a headland, with extensive sea views. Bolam is on a rise, looking across the land to the Simonside Hills. Alwinton is in a particularly beautiful situation on rising ground overlooking the upper reaches of the river Coquet, with Angryhaugh to the west.

Such churchyards contain many stories, record many families and share certain characteristics with others in England, particularly in the symbols that appear on headstones.

Symbolism is a kind of shorthand, with layers of meaning. As we shall see, all periods have their symbols and styles, but this narrative concentrates first on the most common, those of the eighteenth and nineteenth centuries. Today, children who are new to such concepts may ask if pirates are buried there, when they see so many skulls and crossbones. Skull, skull and crossbones, hourglass, spade, pick, coffin, angel head with wings, book, coiled serpent, the Grim Reaper and curtains are all well represented in Northumberland. Death's dart or spear is rare. The headstone at Hartburn includes the rare conch shell, emblem of pilgrimage.

28 Bamburgh: the work of erosion.

29 Alwinton church.

30 Above Hartburn.

31 Right Elsdon.

At Elsdon there is a skull, a curtain looped to form a bag full of long bones, and a winged hourglass.

St Peter's, Falstone, has some particularly interesting stones, including a unique design of a woman in a pleated, spreading skirt, and an indication of hairstyle. She has her left hand on her hip, while the other holds branches with circular rosette-shaped flower heads. To her right stands a skeleton, smaller than the woman, his left hand extended to what might be an hourglass standing on a mound jutting out from the headstone. He may have a scythe (it looks like a staff). Above the semi-circular recess in which these figures are housed are the words *Momento Mori*, and above them is an angel's face flanked by wings. (Colour 27.)

In the same churchyard is a strongly carved headstone that has no-nonsense images in relief: skull and crossbones, spade and book, surmounted by an angel's head and wings (25).

These images are sometimes used to remind us that we are the skull beneath the skin, that if we hope to join the angels we have to live our lives properly. Father Time, the Grim Reaper, waits for us. There is an accidentally decapitated version of him at St Cuthbert's, Elsdon.

The book images may represent many things: Bible, Prayer Book, knowledge, an account of our lives. Sometimes angels may play a trumpet – the trump of

32 Elsdon: The Grim Reaper.

33 Elsdon: William Riddle's grave.

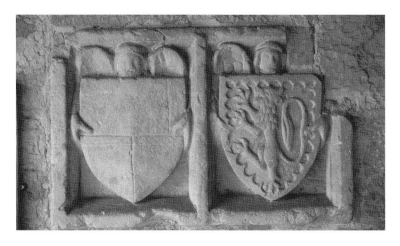

34 Stamfordham: tomb chest with a coat of arms.

doom. With classical revivals came broken columns, reminding us that time is short and we can die suddenly, funeral urns, drapes, sad angel faces, people leaning on pedestals. There may be an anchor of Hope, or a heart of Charity (love).

The pensive lady who adorns William Riddle's grave at Elsdon is a common design.

At its best here, it is also to be seen, for example, at Whitley chapel on a late eighteenth-century headstone.

There is not much heraldry included on Northumberland graves. A good example, protected inside the church, is at St Mary's, Stamfordham. It is part of a fifteenth-century tomb chest, possibly belonging to a knight whose image, with crossed legs, is inside the church.

The place to find some of best and most numerous headstones of the eighteenth century is at St Andrew's, Hartburn. A selection of these follows:

35 Examples of headstones from Hartburn.

Whereas early graves are made from local material, the same as that used for houses, castles, towers and churches, tastes began to change and more exotic stones were imported. Today we see so many different materials, such as granite, slate, alabaster and marble, which would only have been used by the wealthy. In Chillingham, St Peter's church has an out-of-proportion monument in such a small building to Sir Ralph Grey and his wife (1443), made in alabaster on a tomb chest that is profusely ornamented. This is, of its period, of great national interest (Beckensall, 2001, p.40).

Grace Darling became internationally famous after her daring rescue of shipwrecked people off the coast at Bamburgh, and the recently renovated memorial to her in the churchyard there is exceptional.

An unusual and prominent monument for this county is the Hopper Mausoleum at Greymare Hill on the borders of County Durham, perhaps built by Humphrey Hopper for his wife, who died in 1752, but it may have been built by an earlier Humphrey in 1663 (Pevsner, 292).

An outstanding piece of carving is to be seen in Ford St Michael's churchyard, on the grave of Louisa, Marchioness of Waterford (1891). An interesting reflection on fame is that George Culley, one of the most important farmers

36 Grace Darling's tomb before restoration.

37 Ford: Marchioness Waterford's gravestone.

of the eighteenth century, has only a simple slab with his name, in the same churchyard.

Materials such as iron are used mainly for railings around family plots, appearing in the eighteenth century. Iron is used in Warden churchyard to protect graves. Not only would animals try to dig, but there was a real threat of body snatchers, who could make money out of corpses for medical research. For this reason there are some small buildings within churchyards for watchmen, as at Morpeth.

More recent headstones record occupations; when this is accompanied by a picture our interest quickens. There is a splendid headstone at Chollerton erected to John Saint in 1887, a fuller (cloth-maker), described as a 'Dyer and Bleacher', with a picture of the Cocklaw Fulling Mill. John died at seventy-seven, his wife at eighty-one, and their daughter at forty-eight. On the other side it says:

> At Birtley Pit Houses May 22 1889 who died aged 92 years William Saint for upwards of 50 years Parish Clerk and School Master at Humshaugh.

The family enjoyed long life, as the gravestone to the south records Joseph Saint, who died at Cocklaw Fulling Mill on 26 April 1886 aged 102. His wife Alice died at sixty-four, and their daughter aged thirty.

38 Morpeth: watch-house protecting the dead.

39 Chollerton: a pictorial headstone.

In 1874, George Potts, who died aged thirty-four, was buried at Newbiggin beneath a headstone that records his work as clockmaker.

There is a gravestone at Stamfordham with a roundel containing fruit and flowers, a late eighteenth-century memorial to a gardener, Joseph Fothergill.

40
Newbiggin.

41
Stamfordham:
gardener's
grave.

The Newbiggin St Bartholemew's graveyard is remarkable not only for its ancient graves but for the new approach to recording death, for here we have less formal inscriptions, modern materials with a predominance of black backgrounds with pictures of leisure time interests such as golf, football and racing cars. The recording of tragic, early deaths continues in a different way.

At Rothbury is a memorial to 'The Coquet Angler', Walter Mavin, who died in the early 1900s, embellished with plants, a heron and fish.

A pilot and a mason share the same decorated stone at Old Bewick.

Sometimes inscriptions on memorials read like a biography. In St Maurice's church, Eglingham, Henry Baker Tristram, MA, has a plaque erected by 242 of his parishioners, which describes his career through Oxford, his dedication to a vocation as a priest and the principles that governed his life.

A headstone at St Anne's, Ancroft is erected to the memory of Mary Catherine Smith, the Superior of a religious community given lodgings at Sir Carnaby Haggerston's castle for twelve years after the French Revolution.

Words can be used to soften the reality of death. A commemorative plaque to John Appleby of Low Buston in Warkworth church reads: 'He suddenly exchanged mortality for life', with the advice 'Be ye also ready'.

42 Bamburgh: modern memorial.

43 Old Bewick: pilot.

44 Old Bewick: symbols of a Masonic order.

45 Ancroft church.

46 Ancroft: refugees.

One of the saddest headstones was found recently used as paving at a house at the north end of Homers Lane, between Warden and Chesters, with an inscription to 'The Baby', an unbaptised child born dead and presumably not considered for burial in a churchyard. The headstone is now raised outside the house where it was found.

At St Mungo's, Simonburn, the contrast between light and dark is made in this epitaph:

> Tired of travelling through this world of Sin,
> At length I'm come to Nature's common Inn;
> In this dark place here, for to rest a Night,
> In hopes t'rise that Christ may give me light.

There are symbols in church use that do not appear on gravestones. In Hexham Abbey and Warkworth there are pictures of a pelican feeding her young with drops of her blood – symbols used centuries apart, but meaning that just as the pelican was supposed to revive her young by giving them drops of her own blood, so Christ did for us. In fact, the pelican smears oil from its feathers to protect its young.

47 Hexham bench end: pelican.

In Hexham there are three pictures painted on wood (very rare) with John holding a chalice from which a worm or dragon is flying. The story goes that Satan challenged him to drink poison from the chalice, but he made the sign of the cross and was unaffected. The devil fled in anger in the form of a serpent. St Peter holds the keys to the kingdom, and apostles exhibit the instruments of their martyrdom. (Colour 6)

Prior Leschman's tomb is surrounded by many grotesque heads and by symbolic figures that may have come from an earlier period, each with a meaning to those who made or viewed them, such as gluttony and pride. It is clear that in past life, as in the present, symbolism loomed large.

All this is part of a rich survival of Northumberland's past, but it is not the earliest, so the clock will now be put back to look for other survivals. I have dealt with some prehistoric burials and monuments in other works (Beckensall, 2001 (a) and (b), 2003). There are abundant traces of the Romans, and some of their monuments have been recycled into other buildings, such as the crypt of Hexham Abbey and the huge slab dedicated to Flavinus. At Vindolanda, replica tombstones have been set up, which tell their story of the many gods revered and something of the people commemorated.

48 Hexham: Leschman chantry.

The Tyne Valley is rich in Anglo-Saxon architecture and memorials, with many of the 154 fragments listed in the county of various sizes and states of preservation. At Hexham, among others, there are two crosses, thought to be from the head and foot of Acca's grave, that are certainly outdoor monuments. There is a triangular-sectioned grave cover with rounded tiles carved on it to make it look like the house of the dead. Similar graves appear in other churches, such as Warden and Bolam. The Frith Stool of the seventh century, Anglo-Saxon fragments and a scatter of reused Roman stone are also part of the heritage. At Holy Island there are many pre-Conquest stones on show, including the famous one depicting a Viking raid. In the north transept of the priory there is a pre-Conquest cross-base.

One of the great survivals is the Rothbury cross, now split between the Museum of Antiquities and All Saints church, where it serves as the base of a font. It is the earliest stone rood in the country, with Christ crucified on the cross-head, the Ascension, witnessed by crowds of wide-eyed people, spiral scroll, and animals and humans struggling in foliage.

49 Hexham: Flavinus.

50 A replica grave at Vindolanda.

51 Holy Island Priory cross-base.

52 *This page and next page:* Rothbury cross. *All Saints church and NUM*

52 Rothbury cross. *All Saints church and NUM*

One piece of workmanship that dates to the pre-Conquest period with very early origins is at Warden, in the porch. A Roman figure on a massive slab has been reused, with the stone split lengthways to accommodate Saxon motifs as a gravestone. Outside the same church is an early hammer-headed cross, moved into the churchyard from elsewhere.

Peter Ryder has estimated that one third of Northumberland's medieval churches 'have a fabric sharing Saxon style or tradition, which must date them to before *c.* 1100' (Pevsner, 1992).

Some early medieval coffins exist – great slabs of stone hollowed out to fit the bodies of old and young.

There are over 700 medieval grave slabs of the twelfth and thirteenth centuries, best seen in quantity at Bywell and Newbiggin. At St Andrew's, Bywell, some of these slabs used to be incorporated into the outside wall, but most have now been taken inside for their protection. There are twenty-five in all, with fascinating variations. We have male and female symbols, a hunting horn, for example, and a very elaborate ten-armed cross with shield, sword and rampant lion. (Colour 16)

53 Warden: Reused Roman carved stone, with added motifs.

54 Stone coffins, Warden porch.

55 Bywell medieval grave slabs. A man has a sword motif, and a woman a pair of shears.

Many of the slabs have found favour as later building material, as have some even more recent ones. The beautiful late nineteenth century tower at Kirknewton has a baby girl's slab incorporated. So has the north exterior wall of Old Bewick just below a new roof line. Hexham Monastic Workshop has several in alcoves and used as stairs, and Corbridge vicar's tower has another built inside. A Corbridge café has a pair of sheep shears from a woman's grave built into the inside wall, a talking point for the customers. At Edlingham church, male and female slabs with sword and shears lie side by side as a threshold step.

The absence of brasses in memorials is hardly surprising where raids on property were frequent and times lawless. Being Border country, Northumberland had little time to develop the arts; this shows in the emphasis on so many defensive structures, such as towers and castles. What is so good is the way so much of more peaceful times has survived. A darkness falls, but the light breaks through again.

However, for all those who are remembered, there are thousands who have no memorials.

56 Shears.

three

The valley of the shadow of death

DISEASE AND DEATH

There are many things that we fear and have always feared; a particularly frightening prospect is of a sickness that is invisible except in its results. If the sickness is on a vast scale, that fear increases to panic. Plague and cholera are two such sicknesses, and led people to ask why such calamities should befall them. One answer, still given by some in the case of Aids, is that we have brought it upon ourselves through sin. It becomes a stick to beat us into submission to the will of God, or rather to the will of those who think that they know the mind of God better than anyone else.

Even with modern science, we still are unsure of where or how foot-and-mouth disease came into the twentieth century, let alone agreeing on the best way to control and eradicate it. Anthrax sent fear through America and elsewhere, but its purpose as a weapon of terror is different from the spread of such diseases as the plague or cholera in the past.

The effect of disease on society is far-reaching. The Black Death of 1348-9 and its recurrence for many years afterwards was one of the most catastrophic events in history. In England it killed nearly half the population. It is difficult to appreciate what such a statistic meant to families and communities, being almost unthinkable. It struck suddenly, dramatically. There was absolutely no defence against it. An observer in Italy, Boccaccio, of literary fame, gives us this eyewitness account:

In men and women alike it first betrayed itself by the emergence of certain tumours in the groin or the armpits, some of which grew as large as the common apple, others as an egg, some more, some less, which the folk called gavocciolo. From the two said parts of the body this deadly gavocciolo soon began to propagate and spread itself in all directions

indifferently; after which the form of the malady began to change, black spots or livid
making their appearance in many cases on the arm or the thigh or elsewhere, now few and
large, now minute or numerous.

There are some horrifying accounts of its effects on the Continent. In Britain it
is not always possible to get accurate information about its spread and effects, and
not every region was affected in the same way. With such a fall in population, an
immediate result would be a shortage of labour in the labour-intensive industry
of agriculture. There would be a general shortage too of skills. In the short term
there was less demand for food supplies and other goods. Imagine what would
happen on the land: tracts of land became available when there was no one to
cultivate them. Some may have taken advantage not only by upping the cost
of their labour, but also of taking over the land itself as new tenants. If there
were still not enough labour to cultivate the land, some of it could then be
converted to pasture to provide marketable wool, leather and meat for increased
consumption at home and abroad. In the past surpluses had gone to the Church
and to the landed aristocracy, but they suffered death like everyone else. The ones
who already had land could get more, but the peasants benefited by being paid
more; this increased their household wealth and they were able to eat better and
more varied food. This would go on until labour caught up with demand, but it
didn't; there had been too many deaths. Being better off in the country did not
stop people moving into towns, and there was a good chance of finding a job
without the right level of skill for it. This raising of the status of the poor didn't
go down well with everyone; history tends to be written by the better-off, and
they saw the lower orders getting above themselves. This did not end the feudal
system though, despite mutterings about disrespect and moral decay.

A catastrophe like the Black Death had another effect: to make people think
inwardly about their lives. When things are going well they could relax, but the
sight of all those deaths and burials and the thought of their being the next, made
them think more urgently about judgement, heaven and hell. There was plenty
to remind them, for many of their churches carried warnings on their vivid
murals of the perils of hellfire. As many priests, often in the front line as they
hastened to deathbeds to perform the last rites, perished, the normal disposal of
the dead might be abandoned. With no priests available, lay people might have to
say the prayers for the dying. If burial in churchyards became impossible, bodies
might be dumped unceremoniously in mass graves. Not only was it the economy
that was affected; its repercussions reached deeply into many aspects of society.
There was great confusion about what to believe and what or whom to blame.

J.J. Jusserand in his *English Wayfaring Life in the Middle Ages* of 1891 writes:

Faith disappeared, or was transformed; men became at once sceptical and intolerant. It is not
at all the modern, serenely cold, and imperturbable scepticism; it is a violent movement of
the whole nature which feels itself impelled to burn what it adores; but the man is uncertain

in his doubt, and his burst of laughter stuns him; he has passed through an orgy, and when the white light of the morning comes he will have an attack of despair, profound anguish with tears and perhaps a vow of pilgrimage and conspicuous conversion.

Fear of death and uncertainty about the destination of the soul were common to all society. People saw the skull beneath the skin, and funerary monuments have echoed this awareness. Images portray a graphic reminder that death creates equality; it does not matter who you are. All come to judgement when the Reaper calls. This did not prevent a show of ostentation in the funerary monuments of those who could afford it, neither did it bring very much humility.

What about the survivors? An interesting thought is that, with the shortage of labour and the increased prosperity of the survivors, women's roles changed. They were workers too, and could demand more for their work. Some might have lost their menfolk and have become more independent. Three-quarters of the population were labourers and farm workers. Even if the total wealth of the nation declined, there was more per person. From being a society that was based on those who fight, those who pray and those who work, it had become much more fluid by 1500 as wealth changed hands – a change presumably helped along by plague and its effects.

The Peasants' Revolt of 1381 began and spread in the more affluent parts of England, the South East. It was not the very impoverished fighting against oppression, but was led by those who were benefiting from changing economic conditions; they wanted more. The mighty had been struck down from their seats by the Black Death and the humble and meek had been exalted. They turned to the young king Richard II to redress the balance of power in their favour. The huge army that assembled outside London meant business and John of Gaunt, the king's uncle, having fled to the comparative safety of Northumberland, was not allowed into his own castles and fled to Scotland. It is not my intention to pursue this story any further, except to say that the revolt eventually failed; many more died that year. It is symptomatic of the change that had taken place in society, with the adjustment to the balance of wealth leading to a demand for more power.

The scale of the Black Death varied from place to place. Seventy-eight per cent of Jarrow Priory's tenants died, and at Belford in Northumberland the cemetery had to be enlarged to cope with the dead from six surrounding hamlets. The plague spread along the roads and through markets, so no one was safe.

The period of the Black Death is part of the ongoing wars and raids on and in the Borders. Plague continued to flare up in different regions of England throughout the fourteenth century (it was not until the 1520s that the population levels began to recover). An Augustinian canon in Leicester in the late fourteenth century recorded how the Scots in 1348 had massed their forces in the forest of Selkirk to taunt the disease-ridden English, waiting to attack, but caught it themselves and spread it throughout Scotland. The plague carried on, culminating in the Great Plague of London (1665). Where it came from and why it went away is a mystery.

The evidence of its passage is both documentary and archaeological, the latter sometimes coming from the mass graves that accompanied the plagues.

This brief reflection on an ever-present menace to life and its effects on society points to one of the many undercurrents in our history. 'Though I walk through the valley of the shadow of death' was an everyday trial.

In more recent times people have had to cope with other forms of illnesses and have tried to combat them with methods varying from science to superstition. Whereas enlightened people have seen the link between dirt and the spread of disease throughout recorded history, and have understood the importance of good food, fresh air, good sanitation and personal cleanliness to the control of disease, they have not always prevailed.

Sometimes the meaning of much of history is lost. It becomes for some a matter of words and of juggling ideas, putting forward theories, being clever. A 'cool web of language' can remove us from reality. We may speak of disease as something remote, but when we are reminded of what it implies for the people suffering it, it may become real – even from a distance. Take cholera, for example – a word that appears in all the reports soon to be cited. What did it mean to those who experienced it? Its terrible reality was that it began with a sensation of giddiness, unease, anxiety, followed by 'prodigious evacuation, when the whole intestines seem to be emptied at once'. There was a fluttering in the pit of the stomach, tightness of the waist. Limbs became clammy and the heart slowed down. Movement made the sufferer sick. The lining of the intestines came away in motions that were like rice water. The body lost water in a great purge, shrivelling the victim. Cramps followed, with pains like acute arthritis. The features collapsed and the body turned blue or black. Pain could contract the person into a ball and the body stayed like that until death.

The sheer inability of anyone in authority, including surgeons, to deal with this was understandable, but the absurd quackery that accompanied diagnoses and treatment was often delivered by pompous, self-seeking fools. What the sensible realised at the time was that the conditions under which disease flourished could be rectified. What was distressing was that some good people were so pressured that they were forced into positions that they believed were wrong. This certainly happened in the first place where Asiatic cholera arrived in 1831: Sunderland. The port was so dependent on foreign trade that the commercial interests would not accept what was really happening, and press-ganged the professions to declare at first that there was no cholera in Sunderland. That's what many wanted to believe, but no one could deny the horror to which lack of action led. As Charles Greville reported in November, 1831: 'The conduct of the people of Sunderland on this occasion is more suitable to the barbarism of the interior of Africa than to a town in a civilised country'.

Chief among the greedy and stupid was the Marquis of Londonderry, who had a huge financial stake in the coal trade. It was his lead, followed by others, which caused the climb down of the medical profession, when they publicly recanted their professional opinions, and declared one after the other that there was no cholera in Sunderland. This made the town the laughing stock of Britain, as many doctors had flocked there to see for themselves what they would later be facing in their own towns. It also caused the 'lower orders' to ignore any sensible advice that doctors and others gave them.

It was this kind of desperate situation that forms the background to Edwin Chadwick's report presented to the House of Lords in 1842, *Report on the Sanitary Conditions of the Labouring Population of Great Britain*. It resulted in the Public Health Act of 1848, when government for the first time took responsibility for the health of its people. Chadwick was a prodigious worker, but his report had to draw on information from all over the country, the kind of information that is to be seen in the reports on individual towns and villages. It also encompassed factories, prisons, Poor Law, emigration and local government. The great spur was the rapid growth of population in the towns, with pressure on housing leading to back-to-back terraces and the installation of cellars in already overcrowded areas. It was abundantly clear that there was a correlation between overcrowding and disease.

Clean water supplies were crucial; today a litre of water costs five times as much in a Nairobi slum as in an American city, 10 litres of water that flushes a loo in England provides the daily allocation of washing, drinking and cooking needs of a person in the developing world. Water Aid also tells us that 6,000 children die each day from unsafe water and bad sanitation, 1.1 billion people (one-sixth of the world's population) do not have access to safe water, and double that number do not have adequate sanitation. How many of the better-off realise that this is happening?

Bubonic Plague had last struck in 1665. Some diseases suddenly appear, and eventually, for no apparent reason, disappear for a while. Although vaccination, discovered by Jenner, had brought smallpox under control for a while, once the disease waned people forgot about it, until it came back. We see in the Northumberland reports how prevalent it was. Cholera first struck in 1831-2, then in 1848-9, 1854, and 1867. Hundreds of thousands suffered and tens of thousands died. It really scared people because it struck down its victims so quickly. In the end, it went as quickly as it came, aided by better water supplies.

Typhus and consumption were more persistent and enduring. The sanitary report in Edwin Chadwick's document concentrates mainly on typhus – universally called 'fever' – both epidemic and endemic. It was there all the time, but came out in peak times. It was always lurking in narrow streets, closes and courtyards. As an epidemic it appeared from 1826-7, 1831-2, 1837, and 1846. Some noted that it appeared when trade was bad, when people had no work and little hope, and that its growth was related to living standards.

Not all the reports which we see mention consumption (or tuberculosis), but this was a greater killer than cholera or typhus. It was common but little understood, except there was a recognised link between the disease and undernourishment and squalor. Until the end of the nineteenth century it was an urban disease, and became the single most important cause of death after the 1830s.

Some reports, looking for some cause outside their own towns of disease, blamed incomers, especially the Irish, and the Irish Poor Inquiry of 1836 concluded that they 'are frequently the means of generating and communicating infectious disease'. So the incidence of typhus in 1846-7 was blamed by some on Irish migration at the time of the Potato Famine. Others saw that it already flourished in overcrowded and insanitary areas.

To cope with crises, local Boards of Health sprang up, but would disband when epidemics waned. That something more permanent was needed was acknowledged in the Public Health Act; central control or direction had become essential.

The massive growth of towns, concern about working conditions reported by factory inspectors and a new scientific approach to problem-solving were three factors involved in the new awareness that there were serious problems. Florence Nightingale painstakingly collected statistics before and after her hospital reforms at Scutari (1855) during the Crimean War. It was soon realised that there were more deaths from disease than from battle, and that routine nursing care and hygiene reduced death among the soldiers. There was a groundbreaking study in London that involved the careful mapping of all cholera cases in a particular area, with the conclusion that the source was a well. When it was closed, after a lot of fuss, the cholera disappeared.

Parliament and local authorities began to spend a lot of money organising inspections and reports – a sure sign of the awakening national and civic conscience.

A detailed, fascinating insight into conditions in small Northumberland towns is given in a series of Public Health reports in the mid-nineteenth century, which mark the movement away from leaving all matters of public health to local authorities and individuals to some sort of central state control. Overcrowding in industrial towns, filth, disease and moral disintegration alarmed even those who were insulated from such privation themselves. There were great souls who looked in detail at what was happening around them, whose consciences would not let them rest, and who came out of their safe, protected lives to work for their fellow human beings. Prison reform, anti-slavery, votes for a wider range of people, the fight against disease and poverty, the improvement of living and working conditions were all great causes. Lord Shaftsbury, Florence Nightingale and Josephine Butler were among those who fought for a better quality of life for those who could only express themselves by their frustration. Churches took on the fight, some managing to break away from the cosy respectability of established religion. Methodists and Quakers and other dissenters reached the parts of society that others were afraid to enter. Clergymen and doctors working among the poor, often at great risk to their own health, saw what had to be done through radical change.

There were, of course, the fat cats who preferred things to go on as before because they were the main beneficiaries of an exploitation of other human beings. Some ratepayers were reluctant to pay out money towards the improvement of the condition of the poor. They saw the problems of an influx of vagrants, Irish itinerant labour and other 'unsavoury' beings as an added financial burden. Today some of us have the same kneejerk reaction to asylum seekers. They had to be convinced that if conditions of health through better sanitation, water supply and housing were to improve, it would in the end actually cost them less in poor relief. In some Northumberland towns there may have been a kind of local mafia of self-interest that wanted things left as they were. 'The rich man in his castle, the poor man at his gate' was for some the natural order of things, for 'God made them high and lowly'. We have seen this in the memorials of the rich; they expected to carry on their high status beyond the grave. What would Jesus have thought of that?

The Government's response to the enormous problems of the nation was to send inspectors to places where they were invited. They were to report on health by gathering together the opinions of all those who had a voice in the community and by seeing for themselves what sort of conditions people lived in. The spread of disease, especially cholera and typhus, was the trigger, for disease and death were no respecters of persons. The inspection would offer practical assessments on how conditions could be improved, and for how much money. It was then up to the local government to decide whether they should wish the Act to apply to them, which meant central support for their improvements.

The name stamped on the report of inspections is that of Robert Rawlinson, who was to report to the General Board of Health in London.

In the mid-nineteenth century the great concern expressed by many for the health and welfare of so many British people found its voice in Parliament. The result was increasing central intervention, and in particular the establishment of a General Board of Health. It was not just the new industrial towns that bred disease; the countryside was clearly not the healthy place that rosy-cheeked, vibrant milkmaids seemed to epitomise.

The procedure for applying the Public Health Act to any area was to get 10 per cent of the ratepayers to ask for an inquiry, at which interested parties could have their say. Although it was quite obvious that conditions of life were very insanitary for many, those rich enough to be ratepayers were reluctant to part with their money, and were wary of a central authority interfering with their rights to administer their own local affairs. In the examples that I have chosen, the story of inspections and what they revealed becomes very clear.

I have selected reports on the Berwick area, on Morpeth and Bedlington, Alnwick and Hexham: geographically these towns are spread out across the county and have much in common, and these reports throw light on many different aspects of life in them.

To begin with, the borough of Morpeth and the village of Bedlington in a report of 1849. The statutory 10 per cent of ratepayers had requested the General Board of Health to visit, and this was done. Morpeth had 3,441 inhabitants at the time; the borough included Newminster, Stobhill, Tranwell, Hepscott and Bedlington. Morpeth itself had 632 tenements and houses. The report commented on the beauty of the town and its healthy position, and outlined its history and geology.

There were already rules and regulations in force to deal with problems of public health. The emptying of pigsties, privies, night soil, offal, putrid meat or fish, carrion, blood, dung, manure and other offensive matter into the streets and courtyards was punished with fines. People were not allowed to leave any means of transport of themselves or goods lying around.

Offensive material is listed in detail as 'night soil, offal, putrid meat or fish, entrails of fish, carrion, dead animals, blood, dung, manure, oyster shells, bones, broken glass, china or earthenware, dust, ashes, refuse, vegetable, fruit, dirty water or other offensive matter or thing so as to occasion any nuisances or annoyance...'

This also applied to any building materials left lying around in the street; if a house were being repaired, there should be room for people to pass, and a warning light had to be kept burning at night.

57 Morpeth Market, 1832.

There were other regulations. If anyone after 9 a.m. shook or dusted carpets in the street or blocked the streets and pavements with carts, vehicles and tools, they would be fined. There were penalties for breaking lampposts or pipes, kite-flying, skating, bonfire-building and setting off fireworks or firearms. Brawls, disturbances of the peace, window-breaking and the burning of effigies were all breaches of the law. Ferocious dogs that were unmuzzled were not allowed to wander free. People were fined for leaving trapdoors and cellar entrances open, for bill-sticking, indecently exposing themselves and selling obscene and indecent literature. Animal-baiting and dog fighting were forbidden. People were responsible for wandering animals.

Private drains, sewers and footpaths were the responsibility of the owners and had to be kept in good repair. The ratepayers had to pay local taxes for highways, church-rates and poor-rates. To all these points that showed that they were trying to come to terms with problems of cleanliness and health, the locals added that:

> A local sanitary committee has regularly inspected the town, and nuisances have been removed. To this active and intelligent inspection the absence of disease must, in great measure, be attributed.

This part of the report, then, highlighted problems and attempts already to rectify them, but it was not enough. The report made these points: that there were no effective drains and sewers. Privies were close to houses, and in some cases under the bedrooms. The most crowded areas of the town were the dirtiest, with no drains to carry away all the filth, and scarlet fever was prevalent in such areas. The local surgeon said, 'I always find the virulence of the disease proportional to the conditions of the place in which it occurs'. Public lodging houses were particularly bad, especially at harvest time, and there was no fever hospital to treat victims. In the year of the inquiry there had been five cases of cholera in the summer, three of them 'imported'.

One problem for those who had to pay local taxation was that they feared any reforms would cost them a lot of money, but this report and others like it stated that 'a neglected and dirty district is sure to be the most expensive'. Pay now, and benefit later. It was cheaper to buy up dirty property, remove it and build new. The worst areas were pinpointed. Paupers lived together in the same areas of the town in overcrowded conditions. Many of the paupers had been receiving relief for ages.

> These localities had a deteriorating effect on both the morals and health of those inhabiting them, as a large proportion of the illegitimate children whose mothers are natives of this town are born in them and in them also a greater number of children, both legitimate and otherwise, die than in any other parts of the town. The causes of death as registered are convulsions, marasmus, tabes, mesenteria, croup, scarlet fever, whooping-cough, consumption, and in 1847, when these places had nearly doubled their usual amount of

population, owing to the great number engaged in the Newcastle to Berwick railway, typhus fever of a virulent form was prevalent in all of them.

Vagrants were always a problem because of their travelling the Great North Road, moving from one place to another during the year. Scots and English outnumbered the Irish, but the numbers of Irish rose in 1847 because of famine and disease there. Authorities refused to 'relieve' those who were able-bodied. It is no surprise that vagrants came in for particular criticism. They were 'riotous and violent, frequently burning their bedding and doors'. It was shrewdly noted that the expensively built Morpeth gaol accommodated 100 prisoners at an outlay cost of 1000 L (£) each.

> How strange that gaols should cost so much, and sewers and drains for the honest be neglected.

The bad state of drains and sewage disposal 'surrounds the poor inhabitants with a surface of visible filth, and also keeps them in an atmosphere of foul gases, where the seeds of disease most readily ripen.'

The case for spending money wisely was made again, for

> The ratepayers in general are losers, because the sick man must be supported; and if he dies, his widow and young family are too often left as a legacy to the parish. And families so degraded, rarely ever find means of self-support.

The report on Morpeth gives a clear insight into the way people were beginning to see the link between clean water supply, good drainage, better housing and an improvement in health and quality of life generally. Nearby Bedlington came in for investigation because the Act could then extend to the whole borough and not just to Morpeth. Bedlington was developing industrially, with its collieries and an important ironworks, including a locomotive engine works. There were 4,200 people in the parish, and 2,500 in the village. Increased population meant increased overcrowding and acute problems of sanitation. That year, 1849, saw more than the average number of deaths recorded in the village, and cholera had broken out.

A survey showed that the geology of the area was good for new drainage schemes, for there was a good fall from the sandstone rock in all directions, and an abundance of local clay to make tiled sewers and drains. In brief:

> The present state of the condition of the village is very unhealthy… most of the houses are surrounded by stagnant water and dirt… No form of sewerage or drainage exists which is of any practical value.

We are given a picture which is similar to so many others in these reports of privies, cesspools, pigsties and middens crowded behind houses. Single rooms were occupied by large families. There was no control over lodging houses. The proprietor of the Bedlington Ironworks gave evidence of no sewers and no water supply other than pumps or wells. Some wives had to go half a mile to get water in summer. Others endorsed this, giving lots of examples of how disease was caused by lack of clean water and no drainage. There was always typhus in 1845 and 1846. On witness said, 'I have known instances where three married families occupied the same room, having no separate curtains or otherwise: this is very common.'

Between five and twelve people occupied a room 14ft–16ft square (4.27m–4.88m). In lodging houses there might be twenty tramps in one room 15ft square. Some had beds, and others slept on the floor. The local vicar endorsed all this and declared that sickness, overcrowding, immorality and filth went hand in hand. One of his concerns was the burial of the dead:

> There is only one burial ground – the churchyard; this was overcrowded, but an enlargement took place last year. There are no interments allowed inside the walls of the church – not for 40 years.

There was widespread concern about moral degeneracy caused by bad housing, and particularly by lodging houses where there was even less control over what went on there. Particularly problematic was harvest-time. Large supplies of labour were needed at the right time, and Irish and other labourers came in search of work just at the time when fever and diarrhoea were rampant. In the overcrowded rooms was 'a tub filled with vomit and natural evacuations'. Bodies were packed head to feet in the sleeping arrangements on the floor. Occupants were stark naked except for rugs up to the waist – men, women and children alike.

The report goes on:

> But nothing but an actual visit can convey anything like a just impression of the state of the atmosphere; those whose senses are not very nice cannot breathe it with impunity, even for a few seconds, with others two or three inhalations are certain to produce sickness; what then must it be to those who sleep there for hours?

Vice, disease, misery and crime were all engendered there.

The report is not all gloom and doom: at Cresswell, a small village nearby, A.J. Baker-Cresswell had eliminated fever by draining the village. There were many who saw that better conditions for the poor should be accompanied by opportunities for education. They saw the falling-off of the need for manual labour and the need for 'the devices of thought', knowledge of science and the acquisition of skills. They looked to the establishment of reading rooms and recreational areas.

Since the inquiry, cholera broke out in Bedlington, with twenty-seven deaths in twenty-five days out of a population of 2,500. This was not surprising, as the areas where the deaths occurred had no proper water supply and no privies. All around was filth, and it was not the answer for an individual to keep his or her part clean; it had to be done on a large scale.

This report concludes with a summary of points that had been hammered out throughout. The needs were:

A perfect system of sewers and house drains

A full supply of water at high pressure

A good surface pavement to all footwalks, passages, yards and courts

Well-formed and well-cleansed streets, footwalks and roads

The regulation and systematic removal of all nuisances, and cleansing of streets, courts and passages

The regulation of slaughter-houses

The licensing and inspection of common lodging-houses, so as to insure healthy ventilation; a proper and decent separation of the sexes

A full and efficient system of public lights, and all other matters and things which are set forth in the Public Health Act, or which shall be provided for in the Order in Council or provisional Order.

THE REPORT TO THE GENERAL BOARD OF HEALTH ON A FURTHER ENQUIRY HELD IN THE PARISH OF BERWICK–UPON–TWEED

A move now to the far north of the county reaffirms the general picture that we have seen in Morpeth and Bedlington, and adds some more interesting observations on how people were thinking at that time.

Berwick had already had its visit by the superintending inspector, Robert Rawlinson, when he was called back in 1850 so that the recommendations could be applied to the whole borough and not just to the parish. People came from Tweedmouth and Spittal to object to the extension of the Act to those places on the grounds that 'within the last three or four years the inhabitants of Tweedmouth had laid down gas pipes, they had lighted the streets, and three-fourths of the houses in the town were well supplied with water.'

Spittal had also been supplied with water in the last two years. 'As to the drainage of these places, the inhabitants considered the expense would be so great that it would by no means counterbalance the benefits to be derived from it.' They did not want to be tied to Berwick 'on account of the establishment charges principally'.

They were assured that nothing would be done without their consent – a central provision in the Act. So what would persuade them? The first thing was that the three areas were already united into one borough 'for all meaningful and parliamentary purposes'. Any schemes to improve drainage, water supplies, sanitation and roads would benefit by having one expert in overall charge.

58 Berwick High Street and town hall, 1811.

59 Berwick to Holy Island, 1832.

Anything that could get rid of refuse at short intervals would be of enormous value to public health.

On a previous visit Rawlinson had

> found middens which had been kept on the premises, close to the dwelling houses for twelve months; and from all the experience I have had, it is these accumulations in the back yards, kept in confined places, that do the greatest amount of danger in creating sickness and fever. Individuals are powerless to remove this refuse themselves; they do not have the time or the means to do it. But one establishment for the whole district would remove these accumulations at intervals of two or three days.

The borough council had agreed to the Act with scarcely any dissent and members were ready to sign

> with a full sense of the flagrant evils under which this town labours, and that this Act would be the means of saving human life, and saving an amount of sickness and disease which is disgraceful to the richer class of the inhabitants.

The mayor of Berwick weighed in with the argument that in the last year five, six or seven women had been made widows by cholera, so that instead of being supported by their husbands they had to be supported by the parish at an expense of 15 or 20 L. (pounds) a year or more, and that this charge would continue until their children had grown up. It was a familiar argument; clean the place up, make it healthy, get rid of disease, and healthy people do not have to be supported by the ratepayers.

Another recurring theme in these reports was the condition of lodging-houses. Agriculture and some new industries depended partly on itinerant labour, and housing these people created great problems.

In a way, the problem of overcrowded and insanitary lodging houses was the trump card that the report was to use:

> When this Act is applied to Berwick, we shall get rid of all the low lodging houses, with their mass of filth, degradation, and wretchedness; and where will the frequenters of these houses be thrown? They will necessarily be thrown into Tweedmouth, which refuses to have the benefit of this Act. If it was for nothing else other than this, I think they (the ratepayers) ought to embrace it.

To support this argument, a situation that had arisen in Liverpool was quoted. Here the corporation had been able to clear out from cellars and lodging houses 'the vagrant beggars, and hordes of Irish who frequent these places'. And where did they go? To Ormskirk, 13 miles away, forcing the people there to build a hospital for 70-80 persons. Then the warning: 'This, or something like this, will be precisely the effect in Tweedmouth.'

Also to reassure the ratepayers was the statement that the Board of Health existed 'not as a compulsory Board exercising a tyrannical sway over the place to which this Act is applied, but as a Board of Appeal, ready and willing to hear every complaint, and to redress every grievance'. Thus, when new water supplies and drainage were considered, there would be a surveyor appointed who would offer his estimates to scrutiny. The greatest expense would be the initial work, after which the maintenance costs would be low. 'No one shall pay anything which does not confer a benefit upon him or his property.'

The surrounding areas were agricultural and there was a fishing industry, so the people there were concerned that they would be paying for something that did not benefit them. They had been told that they had to pay a quarter of the rate, but did not yet know how much that was.

ALNWICK AND CANONGATE

Today, Alnwick has been designated by one major magazine to be one of the best places to live in England. When I first arrived there in 1966 to teach at the College of Education, housed in the castle, heavy traffic struggled its way through the narrow streets, established in early medieval times, in a way that is now almost beyond belief. Now the bypass has taken traffic around the town, but

60 Alnwick Marketplace, 1822.

more traffic is making its way there since the establishment of the Duchess' Water Garden and the fame of the castle in films, most recently through Harry Potter. Renovation of old, often crumbling property in the town centre has taken place, and it appears to be living up to the accolades. However, in the mid-nineteenth century this would not have been the case. It has been the centre of the power of Northumberland rulers for centuries, with the duke still living there for part of the year.

The report on Alnwick in 1850 stressed once again the importance of the money-saving aspects of the application of the Public Health Act to a town like Alnwick. Some towns had expended thousands of pounds to obtain Acts of Parliament for themselves; this Act would enable Alnwick and its sixty-one parishes and townships in the union to do this together, and thus save money. Rural areas should be included so that all would benefit. Amateurs and individuals could not solve fundamental problems; expertise had to be hired and shared.

An insight is given into how the enquiry worked. Thirteen 'memorials' were put forward expressing their opinions. Of these, four were in favour of, and nine against, the application of the Act. Numbers counted for little, for those in favour were the Duke of Northumberland, Earl Grey, the inhabitants of Alnwick town and the vicar of Shilbottle. This was out of a total of sixty-two people entitled to put their views forward.

Rawlinson put his view: The Act would create a governing body where none existed. All ratepayers were protected individually, and could not be taxed without feeling the benefits. One system for highways and roads would save money. All land was rated at one-quarter of its annual value for charges on it.

How was Alnwick coping with disease? We learn that the outbreak of cholera had led to the establishment of a visiting committee, which went to the homes of the sick twice a day.

> The dead were removed from the crowded tenements as speedily as possible, the sick relieved, medical skill provided, and the terrified relations of the afflicted were comforted and, where necessary, pecuniary relief was afforded.

A good look at this town revealed some very bad spots: crowded housing, narrow passages leading off the main streets, and drainage almost non-existent. Anywhere not covered with buildings was walled to confine refuse for twelve months. Natural drainage passed the liquid filth over the surface and through or under houses. The relationship between these conditions and the spread of cholera was apparent, and these conditions extended to the good sandstone houses that, although attractive and solidly built, had cellars that were always damp because they stood on undrained sites.

Other factors that contributed to this filth were the slaughterhouses and open middens, pigs kept on the premises, foul privies close to houses and middens under bedroom floors. Bad drainage might have been a priority, but so was overcrowding.

One strange feature of this report was a perceived link between disease and weather, with whole tables devoted to this apparent connection. They even considered the possible effect of lightning on the spread of disease. However, those who submitted these observations said that cholera might not have been caused by one thing but that 'its preference for filth and, in persons, for the dwellers amongst filth, the diseased, the dissipated, and the immoral' was crucial.

Those houses that had drains let them run into the streets, as there was no alternative. Much of the rubbish, instead of being collected and used to manure fields, drained through the Alnwick Castle grounds into the river Aln. As for water supply, there were only ten public 'pants', and public and private pumps.

Amid all this, the proper burial of the dead was a cause for concern. The only burial ground in the town was St Mary's, and that was 'quite full'. Since 1848 there had been 171 burials there. A new graveyard was proposed on 5 acres at Alnwick Moor, one half for the established church, and half for the others. It was proposed to borrow the money for it and get it back through the rates over thirty years.

We learn that Alnwick had a gasworks, built in 1825, and forty-eight street lamps.

> That a town is well lighted is of the first importance, whether considered in a social or moral point of view… A lamp tends to the comfort and safety of its inhabitants, and also prevents much mischief and immorality.

When the report returned to the need for drainage and sewerage-removal there was a short discourse on the use of tiles for land and town drainage. Earthenware tiles were thought better than brick or stone. The volume of water and the diameter of the pipes had been investigated to cope with the speedy removal of liquid, solid and semi-solid waste to a reservoir, where it could be converted to fertiliser. Land drains would raise the soil temperature and increase fertility; the duke, Earl Grey, and other landed proprietors had used drain tiles for this purpose.

The report concluded that the Act should be applied to the whole union, as several villages were unhealthy. There was fever, and there was cholera in Amble and Hauxley. Out of twenty-five houses in Boulmer there had been nine deaths from cholera, so the breezy seaside was just as hazardous to health as the centre of a town.

HEXHAM

One of the factors that aroused my interest in public health in the nineteenth century was the accidental unearthing of ancient skeletons outside Hexham Abbey in 1990 during the laying of telecom pipes. I have written about the excavation elsewhere (Beckensall, 2001). What is relevant here is that I began to look more closely at conditions in Hexham Marketplace in the past. Having discovered from excavation that the market had probably been on that spot for centuries, without buildings at its very centre, the whole was surrounded by a mass of buildings that included pigsties, slaughterhouses and privies, built partly over the canonical cemetery. It was Rawlinson's report that filled in so many details not only about the centre of Hexham, but also about conditions in adjoining areas, especially Cockshaw, which the Local History Society studied in detail. There was Hexham's main industry – tanning – and particularly the manufacturing of gloves (known as Hexhams tans). Recent work by Anna Rossiter added considerably to the picture in the seventeenth century (about which very little work has been done) and David Jennings' research took him into a consideration of public health later than the Rawlinson report.

Although many of the same themes that we have seen above in reports on other small towns are echoed in the Hexham document, there are interesting additions.

The report was published in 1853. The inquiry took place after 152 people had requested it, out of a population of 2,982. We are told that notice was given via the press and by fixing notices to the doors of churches and chapels. The report gave a brief history and accounts of the geology and meteorology. In giving account of rainfall, the relevance of this to drainage and sewerage was pointed out. An account of the modern town showed it to be crowded, unplanned, dirty and 'not conducive to the health of the inhabitants'. More detail followed.

If we stand in the marketplace today and look west towards the abbey, the picture is very different from 1853. It is relatively uncluttered, with the east end of the abbey open to the town. The wall that divided priory from town has long gone, and so have buildings which until recently crowded the abbey to the east and south. Beaumont Street, with its fine stone buildings that cut right through the abbey grounds and the canons' cemetery, was not built at the time of the inquiry. The plan showed there was a passage from the market to a large yard (the Long Yard) where there were four slaughterhouses and their offal heaps, twelve piggeries, a stagnant drain, a large ashpit and two privies for twenty families, where refuse was allowed to collect for months (Beckensall, 2001). Contrast that with the picture today.

The report says that in the marketplace:

> on the west and north no conveniences at all exist, not one inch of ground to use as a
> yard... In one instance the entire refuse of a family is deposited in a cellar immediately

61 Hexham Marketplace with the pant.

beneath the post-office, so that the whole town is brought within range of its infectious influence... On the south and east sides of the Market-place are to be found, in the generality of cases, small yards containing an area 5 or 6 feet square, and having ashpit and privy. On all sides the yards are surrounded by high walls, so that however much the wind may blow without, within the contaminated precincts no breeze ever comes.

Yet the lie of the land, sloping down to the river, should have made good drainage possible.

A local sanitary report summed up the situation:

Hexham, although possessing every natural advantage for cleanliness and healthfulness, has, by its construction, been rendered comparatively filthy and unhealthy.

If the area immediately around the market was bad, Gilligate (Gilesgate) was worse. Several groups of houses had no privies, and those that did were shared by many families, no one taking responsibility for keeping them clean. A particular horror is described there:

In one instance the drainage from a piggery, privy and ashpit has found its way into the room of an adjoining house, and liquid oozes through the wall, and runs down from the second to the first floor, in such quantity as to wet the beds. A well has been sunk in the room several feet deep, in which these pestiferous drainings are allowed to accumulate until it is full, and then they are removed to make way for more.

Where there were drains, as at Black Bull-bank (now the road with the Forum cinema in it), the five drains that opened onto it formed a stagnant pool at the bottom.

The structures intended for drains are, except in very wet weather, reservoirs, so that almost constantly, from every opening, but especially from those in the vicinity of a water-closet, exhale very offensive and injurious effluvia. The sanitary condition of Hexham is of the lowest class. The few attempts that have been made to improve it, have been too paltry and unconnected to be of much use; they have been made for individual rather than for public good, hence their inutility, and in many instances ultimate injuriousness.

There had been a recent epidemic of smallpox which:

afforded ample proof that in overcrowded and low damp houses in the neighbourhood of offal heaps, disease finds its most numerous victims, and there operates with the most deadly effect.

In one house with forty people living there, thirteen caught smallpox and twelve of these cases were from two families. At the end of Fore Street, one of today's main shopping streets, there were ten cases near to a yard where 'slaughter houses, piggeries, dung-heaps, stagnant putrid pools, and all the other filthy concomitants are crowded together beneath the windows of a row of houses that are parallel therewith.'

The market, being a focal point for agricultural trade, included beasts, and in addition to large numbers of slaughterhouses was the meat market, still known as 'the Shambles' in the town centre.

One imagines that the local doctors would have linked disease to such bad conditions, but there are instances (especially when cholera came to Sunderland in the 1830s, later to spread all over Britain with devastating results) when local practitioners denied the link. Why? Sometimes financial considerations, anything that interfered with trade or anything that was going to cost more in taxes, made some people close their eyes.

One surgeon, Thomas Jefferson, who had seen only one case of cholera in 1831 and 1832, admitted there 'is generally more or less fever', but no more than anywhere else, and 'thinks if the Public Health Act was in force, the sanitary condition of the town could not be improved'.

Mr Robert Stokoe, who had practised for forty years and was the senior surgeon in Hexham, admitted epidemics of smallpox and scarlet fever, but 'I have always considered the town healthy, being seldom visited with contagious or infectious diseases, and never of long duration'.

He considered that proof of this was that people came to stay in Hexham for their health. He blamed local deaths on 'the influx of sick strangers', thought that the mortality figures had been taken from selected periods when disease was rife, and said that the smallpox prevailed among the unvaccinated. William Angus Temperley, a corn merchant, countered with: 'If the town is so healthy as they describe, the average mortality ought to be lower.' Mr Thomas Stainthorpe, surgeon and medical officer to the union, 'considers the town very unhealthy. Attended 217 cases of small-pox during the last winter.' He proved his point by producing statistics to show where smallpox was prevalent in the winter of 1851 and 1852. He arranged the statistics into the five administrative 'wards' of Hexham. Gilligate had ninety-six cases, and this area included the crowded tannery areas of Cockshaw and Tyne Green. Priestpopple (originally the land owned by priests) had forty-one. Market Street and the marketplace area had twenty-five cases. Hencotes (including Back Street, Battle Hill, Victoria Place and West Spital cottage) had thirty-four cases. The Hexham Union Workhouse had twenty cases. All told, this made 216. In seventy-one cases of fever Gilligate had thirty-four during the past two-and-a-half years. He also mentioned that in 1849 five or six cases of Asiatic cholera occurred in Hexham, and the situation was saved by a general meeting of townspeople that arranged for food, bed and body clothing.

In view of the adverse reports on Hexham, it is difficult to understand why anyone should have been against making the changes proposed to improve the cleanliness of the town and for providing it with an adequate supply of clean water. There seemed to be more opposition in Hexham to change than in the others dealt with in this chapter. Three hundred and two people signed against it, and of these 188 were from Gilesgate! The reasons they gave were:

> There are no less than 16 public and open pants and fountains in the town, constantly supplied with a sufficient quantity of water; and, together with the supply of water from private pumps, is more than adequate.
>
> The town of Hexham, from its peculiar situation, has always been, and still is, unquestionably one of the most healthy towns in the kingdom.
>
> The nuisances from time to time recurring in the town, and any want of sanitary regulations, are amply provided against by the powers vested in the Board of Guardians and other local authorities, the said nuisances being in themselves comparatively insignificant.
>
> We further find, that many of the parties signing the petition to the general board of health were, by the propositions held out at that time, led to believe that the measure was one of a trifling nature.

To summarise: Hexham is one of the healthiest places to live, there is plenty of fresh water, we can cope with nuisances ourselves, and you people who signed the petition don't know what expense you are letting yourselves in for.

The report on Hexham has more detail than those already discussed, including details of the gasworks. Other reports include the burial of the dead. Today the main burial grounds used at the time of the report have been landscaped. A walk from the marketplace past the abbey on the north side has a raised area to the north where most of the town's dead were buried, but is now without the mass of gravestones. A sub-committee reported that if each grave were allowed to occupy six feet of space, there was room for 1,965 graves. The population entitled to use the space was 5,528. The average number of burials per year was 120, and if this continued it meant that each grave would have to be reopened every fifteen years or more frequently to bury more bodies.

> It is indeed often very unpleasant to witness the remains of bodies dug out of the ground before they have become sufficiently decomposed. Until three or four years ago the usual depth of the graves was 3 feet, so that the top of the coffins would be scarcely 2 feet from the surface, a circumstance which could not but prove injurious to the health of the inhabitants residing in the immediate vicinity of the churchyard.

They changed the practice and made the depth of the grave five feet. Of more concern was the

> custom, still resorted to by some families, of making use of the inside of the church as a place of interment... there are nearly fifty families which have availed themselves of this privilege during a comparatively recent period of time.

The issue was not straightforward, as people wanted to be buried near their relatives and regarded this as their right irrespective of the danger that it posed. The solution was that a new graveyard had to be found, and that no one should be buried in the church.

Just as people found bones strewn around the burial ground, this still happens when any excavation work is being done in that part onto which the Market Street houses back. Another burial ground was in the place now occupied by the abbey nave where poorer people were buried. Since 1850 there must have been many bones of all periods disturbed, removed, dumped or reburied with the various rebuildings and modifications made to the abbey. The most recent was our reburial of the bones of the canons disturbed by the external 'floorscaping' around the abbey from 1990 onwards, under the floor of the north transept.

Water supply was examined in detail, as this was a crucial factor in the spread of disease. The inspectors did not think that Hexham had paid enough attention to it. The old pant-head system had been in existence since 1800, without providing sufficient or clean enough water. Pants, wells and pumps together provided 36,000 gallons, or 8 gallons a day per person. This was less than

62 Spring-water supply beside the Cockshaw Burn.

Nottingham, Liverpool or Hartlepool. Less than that 8 gallons was used because much of it escaped from the pants. If a service pipe were made available, all the supply could be used. Its quality was also poor, and the pant-head supplies could only be used for washing. It had to be purified, for near the source of the supply were brick and tileworks pouring muddy refuse into the burn. Further on were fields with cattle: more pollution. It thus reached the pants unfiltered.

> It cannot but be wondered at that a town pretending, and not without reason, to a considerable amount of intelligence, should have so long allowed itself of an all-important necessary of life to be furnished by such rude, absurd, and vicious methods.

They found that sudden showers made the water unusable in the pants; the one in Gilligate had a deposit of 4in of mud. The answer to this was house service at high pressure through a public waterworks, and that would cost only a little more than the existing unregulated system. The old committee had to go, although they had done their best with 'a bad system and small funds'. The construction of a reservoir above the town was proposed, and the harnessing of water supplies in springs could add to the water flowing through main pipes. One of the springs

63 A newly uncovered well during house underpinning. *Hexham Courant*

remains just beside the Cockshaw Burn today. As for the pants, the inspectors were not insisting on their closure, but pointed out that other towns had got rid of them because they encouraged servants and others to congregate there!

From time to time when modern building work is undertaken, a little more of Hexham's history is revealed. On one occasion when a large house was being underpinned at the entrance to the Wentworth complex, a well appeared. A similar one appeared at Corbridge in the garden of a house and the latest was to the south of the town, again in a garden, overlooking the middle school field. From the plan of the town which is included with the report, there are many wells marked, representing many private water supplies. No doubt some of those who owned them were not too concerned about other people's right to clean water.

On a lighter note, some particulars 'as to the ancient government of the town' were furnished by Jasper Gibson Esq., solicitor, which were found to be 'nearly useless'. Among them is the Ale-taster's Oath, which goes like this:

> You shall swear, that you shall well and truly serve our sovereign Lord the King, and the
> lord and lady of this manor, in the office of ale-taster or assisor [*sic*] of this town for this

64 Old houses in Gilesgate, now demolished.

year to come. You shall have diligent care during your time of office, to all the brewers and tipplers within your office, that they and every of them do make good and wholesome beer and ale for man's body, and that the same be not sold before it be assayed by you, and then to be sold at agreeable to the prices limited and appointed by the justices of the peace; and all faults committed or done by the brewers or tipplers or by any of them you shall make known and present the same at this court, where due and condign (*sic*) punishment may be inflicted upon them for such their offences accordingly, and in every other thing you shall well and truly behave yourself for this year to come. So help, &...

Once the Northumberland towns had been visited by inspectors and recommendations had been made, we ask the question: did it make any difference? In many dramatic ways it did, especially in pinpointing the cause of disease and its spread, but we have today still not achieved ideal conditions.

There was an outbreak of cholera in Hexham in 1853. Henry Woods, lodging in Holy Island, died. Three more cases followed: two were fatal. Cleansing took place in the form of hot lime and brushes. Streets were washed and swept, and home visits were arranged. More people died, and there were hundreds of cases of diarrhoea. A recommendation that pigsties should be removed was circulated.

One of the board's medical officers was sent from London and, although he tried to be kind to the medical profession, he was critical that there was no regular system for getting rid of nuisances. He wrote:

The town of Hexham is almost entirely unprovided with sewers. There is only one and scarcely any houses have connections with that. The ordure, filth of all sorts and ashes are collected in large pits and bins, and from the approaches to these being too narrow for a cart to enter, their contents are carried out to the street, and remain there till the carts pass to carry them away.

Much lime-washing had been done, but the place was still filthy. He regarded many of the rooms that he visited 'unwholesome and unfit for human habitation'. People in the town, however, were strongly asking for change, though a vociferous group was still fighting against it. They lost, and in 1854 a Local Board of Health was appointed. The final death toll for cholera was twenty-three.

David Jennings' research into Hexham (Jennings, 1998) investigated two reports, one in 1872 and another in 1935 with the follow-up in mind. What follows is based upon that work.

The General Board of Health was succeeded by the Local Board of Health, and then by the Urban District Council in 1894. To their reports can be added the results of Census returns, for these particularly revolutionised the amount of information we have about who was living where, where they were born and what their occupations were. The Census of 1921 was the basis for a report by the Medical Officer of Health to the Urban District Council, which said that 1,721 people out of 8,843 were living in three or fewer rooms. That, of course, is a statistic and does not convey what people experienced as a result of overcrowding. Reports of 1872 and 1935 are very similar in their findings, so what had been done over sixty-five years? Was it a lack of money or a lack of interest, or both?

The report to the Urban Sanitary Authority by John Hodgson in 1872 is certainly similar to the Rawlinson report of 1850. A description of a privy in the upper floor of Victoria Yard, Battle Hill, says that it was in a 'very foul condition', not fit for any person to use. It had no proper seat and was dangerous for children, with filthy matter lying around, oozing through the wall into the premises.

> This is the sole accommodation for about 70 people including the occupants of three lodging houses. The yard is strewed about with nauseous filth; there is no proper drainage and it is seldom swept. There is an ashpit but most of the refuse is thrown upon the open yard. I believe the lodging houses are not registered and are on this account illegal.

He recommended that the ashpits in the whole block should be done away with or reduced in size, and that water closets should replace privies. Mr Matthew Smith, who owned the property, was served notice. It turns out that he was a member of the Local Board of Health and its first chairman (from 1854-1866)! In this case he complied, but his property at what is now Pudding Mews had to have another order served on it.

S.P.B. Mais (1935) wrote *England's Pleasance*, an account of a journey which began at Hexham – 'an admirable starting point because it contains outstanding examples of North-country beauty and North-country wretchedness.' When the driving force behind an unemployed men's club in Haugh Lane took him up Gilesgate to the then-modern post office he was handed three antiseptic lozenges before entering a dark narrow alley that led to a stone courtyard.

> A woman stood outside a doorway turning the handle of a mangle. Dirty water squeezed its way from the mangle over her feet and over the feet of several tiny children who coughed unhappily as they stood in the icy wind just looking at the stranger. He climbed wooden stairs, and at the top of the fourth flight he thought he had been transported into a scene out of *Oliver Twist*.

A woman showed him the bed where she, her husband and five children slept. They were trying to get out of this miserable room into a council house. There were three lavatories in the block for eighty people, and two didn't work. The houses had been condemned ten years ago, 'and yet I was in a stone's throw of the Abbey, and looking out over one of the greenest valleys in England'.

We know that the anecdotal does not make a general rule, but we ask whether all people in the town saw this picture. A letter in the *Hexham Courant* in 1930 from an indignant resident deplored medical officers' reports which drew attention to anything unhealthy in the town. Why?

> There is no doubt whatever that Hexham has sustained considerable pecuniary loss solely attributable to these reports. And those ratepayers whose only means of making a living are entitled to protection and to receive every encouragement from elected councillors and paid officials.

Despite his protestations, there was no doubt that mortality figures from 1920 onwards were very high.

A survey by a group of local historians of the Cockshaw area of Hexham included recollections by people living in that area at the beginning of the last century. The figures quoted in slum clearance reports came to life with people's memories of living conditions in the 1920s and 1930s. Many huge families lived in two or three rooms, with several families to a house. Communal street life was necessary, as there was no room in the houses. Lodging houses were still common. Several people described the dubious characters who lived in them. One Cockshaw resident spoke of her fear of passing the tenement called 'The Mystery'. She and her friends would pluck up courage to dash past the entrance.

65 One site of Hexham tanneries and wool processing at Tyne Green.

The census shows a high proportion of people in lodging houses were from outside Hexham, particularly from Scotland and Ireland. Many people have described Cockshaw as one of Hexham's toughest areas, where several notorious characters lived. Fights between the patrons of adjacent pubs, the Tanner's Arms and the Skinners Arms seem to have been a regular Saturday-night feature.

The bad smell of the burns was frequently mentioned. When the leather industry was operational the water was described as being a thick yellow-brown sludge with a sickly smell that hung over everything. However, despite these problems, there was a great sense of community there. Many families were poor yet were prepared to share what they had. Extended families were common, with married children living close to their parents, providing security for the children. There were no latchkey children, as there was always a relative or friend to help out. Doors were rarely locked. Although the houses were crowded, land by the river at Tyne Green provided a 'back garden' for them to play in.

All this is anecdotal, and one has to balance sometimes conflicting accounts based on individual experiences. This was the same area described in detail in Rawlinson's report. It came in for a slum clearance scheme; a large area of Gilesgate was declared 'an insanitary area' that required a radical scheme. In the Gilesgate ward the density of population was 11.1 per acre, compared with 1.7 in

66 The site of the new Hexham General Hospital when the cattle market was still there. The estate was the result of clearances in the 1930s.

the urban district, but the area with Holy Island at its centre had a density of 186 per acre. Disease was therefore much more prevalent there. They allowed forty-eight properties to remain, and demolished the rest in 1935 and 1936. As a result of these clearances and others in Hexham, large numbers of council houses were built at the east end between the two world wars to rehouse the families. Beside them has now been built the large new Hexham General Hospital. It is only very recently that the tackling of drainage problems at Cockshaw has resulted in expensive and far-reaching public works there.

67 The new hospital before the clearance of the remains of the old. *M. Hutchinson*

four

Shadows of an industrial past

Land has traditionally been the basic source of wealth in Northumberland. There are, of course, many other sources in trade and industry but, in the past, a rich country estate was the outward and visible sign of prosperity and power. When people made money in industry, some, like Lord Allendale and Lord Joicey, immediately bought land. Before the North East became one of the most important areas of industrial development in the world, there were already industries such as coal mining and lime extraction. Add to that the potential for iron and steel production and industries such as glass, and the brainpower and inventiveness of many people, and the scene was set for a transformation of the eastern region of Northumberland. The coastal strip, with its accessibility by river and vast deposits of coal, placed the area in a particularly favourable position for expansion.

Times change, and much of that coal industry has disappeared, leaving communities that were dependent on it bewildered and searching for other ways to make a living. Their past has attracted historians and those who would capture part of it physically as museums for posterity. It has left a changed landscape, and much has been re-formed into an 'acceptable' environment.

In the hinterland of Northumberland there are other signs of industries that are settling back into the earth, unless there is a conscious effort to maintain them.

For some, nothing can be more frightening than the thought of going into the earth. Caves are bad enough, but the prospect of having to earn a living through mining may be unthinkable: claustrophobia, danger, going into the dark are real fears. For many, going into this shadowland was necessary, for this was how they could earn their living. Coal mining has received a great deal of interest and research by historians, and lead mining is now receiving its due. Both industries brought enormous prosperity for some, especially those who owned the land in which the minerals were lodged and the capitalists who financed them.

Such is the nature of change that we have to import coal today and live with abandoned lead workings. Woodhorn Colliery is a kind of shrine, yet there is still coal being mined at Ellington and in opencast mines along the coast. There are a few wind turbines at Blyth, but there is resistance to alternative energy when it impinges on our view. Although people like Lord Armstrong in the late nineteenth century warned about the diminishing reserves of coal and advocated such alternatives as solar power, this was never taken seriously. North Sea oil and gas came as a solution to some of the energy-supply problems, but nuclear power over the border in Cumbria has come to be seen as a Frankenstein's monster.

When industries die they leave a mark in the memory, in memorabilia, in literature and in the landscape itself. Waste is flattened or resculpted. A dangerous legacy persists, for old shafts and galleries continue to pour noxious substances into streams and rivers. Shilbottle, once a producer of high-quality coal, posed all sorts of problems after its closure, and a flight over the site now shows clearly a series of tanks and filters that process the water before it enters the river Coquet.

Communities have died, and no matter what new industries are brought in to substitute, they are never the same. The planned terraces of Ashington with their numbered streets and uniform gardens house people whose lives are no longer tied to coal mining. One particularly poignant survival of the mining era is the intensely individual painting of the Ashington pitmen.

68 Air photograph: filtration tanks at Whittle, Shilbottle.

In the Pennines the impact of industry has left an intriguing mark on what is largely an empty landscape. Some of the mines are being investigated and being made ready for visitors to show something of what it was like in the past. The ripping out of minerals to feed smelters was extensive throughout the limestone strata; the heaps and gashes are there for us to see. So are the chimneys at the end of tunnels, which delivered toxic fumes from smelters to a safer distance away from hearths. These tunnels and chimneys are some of the most dramatic and eerie relics of a defunct industry.

Stubblick's coal mine lies close to a huge stone-and-brick chimney and its flue, away from the little settlement of Langley, which housed the smelter. Three ruined but preserved chimneys rise above Catton, where a garage now lies on the site of smelter and railway, with multiple flue tunnels running from there up the hill to a great viewpoint.

There is another aspect: the crumbled remains of houses and 'shops' scattered over hills and valleys, where miners and their families lived as close as possible to their work. Here they were in another world of fresh air, and some had gardens where they could grow food and keep an animal or two – in the same way that coal miners valued their allotments. The men may have travelled to their work each week and stayed at a lodging house in cramped conditions, but at the weekend many were small farmers or crofters, living with their families and going to the local chapel.

69 Stubblick old coal mine.

70 Catton chimneys before restoration.

71 Catton flue above ground.

1 Inside the Cheviot Hills

2 From Cartington Carriageway to Simonside

3 From Cartington carriageway to the Cheviot Hills

4 Ford churchyard

5 Holy Island Priory erosion

6 Hexham Abbey: John,
chalice and dragon

7 Hexham Abbey: Flavinus

8 Roman wall country

9 Chesters Roman bridge foundation

10 Angerton Station (Birtley Aris)

11 Longwitton Station (Birtley Aris)

12 Langley Station (Birtley Aris)

13 Langley Station – now a garden centre

14 Hexham Abbey: guardian of
the Leschman Chantry tomb

15　Corbridge church west

16　Bywell grave slab

17 Hexham Abbey: Smithson's screen

18 Branxton churchyard to Piper's Hill, Flodden

19 Lambley viaduct

20 Tosson Tower

23 Edlingham viaduct and castle

21 *Opposite above* The Great Hall, Warkworth castle

22 *Opposite below* Catton chimney; outlet for lead-smelting flues

24 Warkworth Pageant

25 Warkworth Pageant

26 Roughting Linn prehistoric rock art

27 Falstone churchyard

28 and 29 The past in the present: work by pupils at Greenfield Community School.

72 Catton flue below ground.

It is this past world that I shall try to enter, basing it on what is still visible in the Pennine landscape. It will not be a comprehensive account, but it will attempt a general picture of life in the late eighteenth and most of the nineteenth century.

The Pennines are billed as an Area of Outstanding Natural Beauty. That is only a part-truth, for much of the landscape has been moulded and used in the pursuit of mineral wealth. By the end of the nineteenth century, most of the operations had shut down.

Lead is extracted from galena, which occurs in veins in limestone – a geological process in which minerals seeped into cracks and fissures. Generally the veins are vertical, unlike coal seams. In many ways they are unpredictable as to where they will occur. The first step was to get the ore-bearing rock out of the ground, the work of miners usually working in teams that arranged for their conditions of work and payments in 'bargains' struck with the owners and their agents. The miners' techniques were largely sheer physical effort and experience. The early means of finding the veins of ore was through 'hushing', in which a body of water was built up through dams high up the hillside, then released. This washed away the topsoil and revealed the mineral veins. An early way of following the ore was to dig a series of pits along its course, deep enough

73 Pennine landscape from the Hexham-Alston road.

to extract ore but not too deep to compromise safety, rather like bell pits in coal mining. Another way was to dig a horizontal shaft to reach the vein and to work upwards. The tunnel had the advantage of admitting a horse and wagon and making a drain.

Miners did not use drills usually, except to bore holes for explosives, but worked with pickaxes and sledgehammers. Rock was also blasted, but this created dust and fumes; sharp particles of rock could be breathed in by the miners and damage their lungs. There were fewer chances of major accidents than in coal mines, where explosions of gas were perilous; in lead mines candles and smoking were safe underground. One of the heaviest tasks was to remove the non-productive rock, known as 'deads'.

At first miners were paid by results, and consideration was given to the difficulty of digging the ore out and its quality, so there wasn't a standard payment. The lead ore arrived from one group of miners as a 'bargain' at a 'bowse', to be weighed and checked in before it was washed. As the big mining companies developed the industry, the men became more tied to wages, but they still worked in teams.

The next stage after mining was 'washing' and breaking the ore into small pieces. Imagine how cold this was in the winter, when the work floor was in the open. When ice formed, work had to stop. Water was a key element, for the sieves and settling tanks needed great volumes of it to keep the process going. The same water was crucial for driving engines too. The process was designed to make use of every piece of ore, no matter how small; sieve and sift again and again.

To keep the whole operation going there were craftsmen needed, particularly blacksmiths and carpenters. To keep the ore moving from mine to smelter there had to be transport, mainly in the form of Galloway packhorses, as the roads initially were appalling and rail transport was slow to come. People involved in transport did not have to live among the miners and smelters.

Smelters formed another category of worker. Basically the ore had to be cooked and the liquid lead siphoned off. Some of it was resmelted to make silver. We know where these smelt mills were, but apart from some bumps and dents in the ground and a few broken buildings there is little left to see. The flues and chimneys have survived well, and make an impressive landscape feature. It was realised that lead fumes were not only unpleasant, but also toxic, and it was important to the smelt workers on the floor and to the people living in the area that the fumes should appear as far away from the mill as possible. One of the best-restored chimneys is at Stubblick next to an old colliery, where it dominates

74 Allenheads: smelt site (old postcard).

75 Allenheads: smelt mill site today.

the road from Hexham to Alston. Originally the Langley smelt mill was one of the greatest producers of lead, with reservoirs and a railway line still there, not far from a medieval tower, but its character today has been changed. There is a sawmill now, with some stone houses.

At Allenheads, multiple flues can still be traced up the hillside from Dirtpots on their way towards Killhope. Again, there are traces of reservoirs, but the remains of buildings on the site of the smelter are confusing, so it is difficult to decide how it all worked. Nearby, the houses are spread alongside the main street, flanked by the remains of mine shafts. Everywhere there are heaps of spoil and quarries, and there is a good limekiln. There will be more about this community further on in this account.

One is constantly aware of what is missing from these landscapes today – people. Of course people live there today, but in much smaller numbers. Some earn their living locally, but others have come in from the outside for a different kind of life from modern urbanisation. They bring money to renovate property that would otherwise have tumbled to earth. They are not depriving young people of a place to live, for not many want to live there any more. Winter lasts too long.

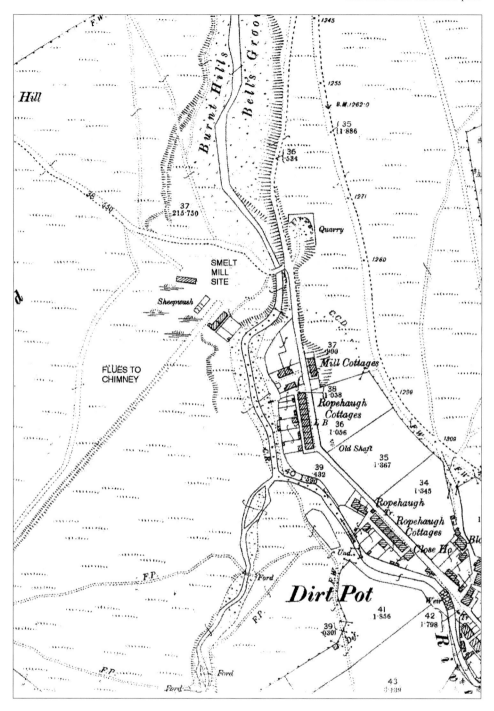

76 Allenheads in the 1860s. *(Flues and smelt mill site added)*

A sprinkling of chapels, derelict places of work and homesteads have to find alternative use. The roads there are mainly those built in the late nineteenth century to overcome some of the horrific transport facilities, which isolated communities in one way, yet drew them closer together in another. Elsewhere there are ghost tracks, used by packhorses. Today, grouse butts represent another fringe industry, in which people pay highly for what the miners might have poached in the past. It seems a strange entertainment to many of us. On the whole this is a harsh land, not at all the kind of rural idyll that some may expect. It is a lonely and disturbing land, saddened by its past. Take away the modern comforts of those who live there, and it might become unbearable, unless they have a special affinity for vastness, emptiness and a haunting raw beauty. As it is, the visitor views it from the security of a car or bus window, which is not the same as becoming part of it, even for a short while.

So what about people who made it their living in the eighteenth and nineteenth centuries? Wherever possible, the mineworkers used the land around their houses as allotments or smallholdings to supplement their diet. When there was work and prosperity, food would be bought in, but a plot of garden and a cow would be an invaluable supplement. There is very little rich arable land; the

77 An Allenheads family group, late 1930s. George Sparke, holding the horse, was a lead miner and farmer who lived for many years without part of a lung, which was damaged in the mine. The man with the moustache, his father Ralph, was also a miner and farmer and died aged eighty-two in 1952. His daughter Lizzie is on the right, and the small blonde girl, her daughter, is the owner of this photograph, taken probably at Sinderhope. *Mrs E. Common*

best is in the valleys. At such a height above sea level there is a restricted growing season. There is scarcely any sign of activity in prehistoric times, so this land has always been marginal agriculturally. Yet lead workers lived high up in the hills, but managed to keep animals. There did not appear to be a separate farming class, the lead workers taking on that role themselves.

These smallholders looked after cattle, cut hay for winter fodder, stored it and cut peat for fuel or, in some cases, exploited small local coal seams. The size of the holdings was between 1 and 10 acres, but most had less than 5. Houses were built of stone, roofed with slate, stone slabs or thatch. The isolated farm buildings were of two storeys; the ground floor had a living room and kitchen all in one at one end and a cattle shed at the other. The family had beds on the upper floor above the living room, and there was a hay loft above the cattle shed. When Greenwich Hospital built the smelt mill at Langley in the 1760s they discussed in some detail the kinds of houses that should be built there. Once the houses were built, the smelters demanded allotments and farm buildings. Some of them had already started to keep cows on the commons. Land was taken from tenant farmers and let to the cottagers. Byres were then added to the cottages. There was not enough land for all, so the skilled refiners were given the first choice; lots were cast. The early nineteenth-century map (p. 104)shows how small enclosures were arranged. Some upland pasture was reserved for common use. The map was made before the railway was built and shows the arrangement of the smelt mill before the building of the flue.

D. Macrae, writing an article on 'The improvement of wastelands' in 1868, in referring to how the men and children were allowed a holiday for the hay harvest, says this:

> Occupations of this sort give the men something more than grooves, ore, lead, washing and smelting, to talk and think about: in short, they become small farmers as well as miners, and so far as my observations have gone, interest themselves wonderfully in the practice of agriculture; so that in the intelligent management of their meadows and stock they compare favourably with professional farmers in some parts of the country.

At Allenheads, settlements grew as the working population increased. The maps show this happening between 1800-1861.

We see more common land being enclosed. At Nenthead the London Lead Company built houses for letting and made land available for building on. This was a different picture from Allendale, where there was already an established village built as a market centre. After 1860 the problems of housing workers were no longer an issue as more and more people were forced out by the death of the industry.

The urge for smallholdings was made stronger by the distance from markets and agricultural areas, but these were only to supplement food availability. Milk and cheese were important items that came from their own animals. Potatoes

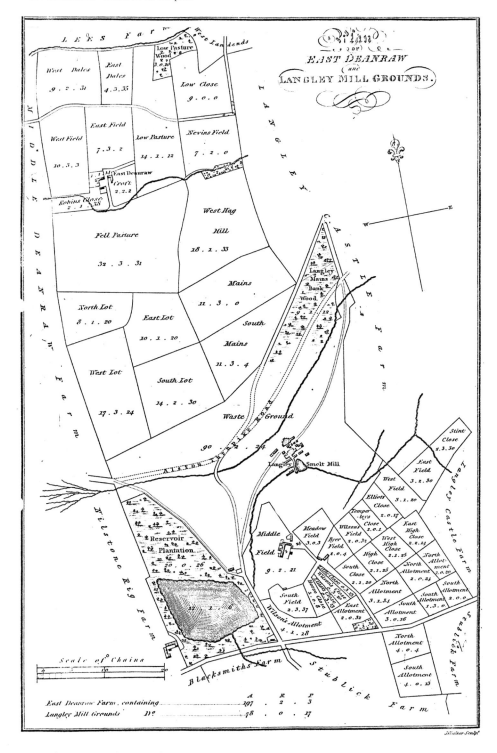

78 Langley Greenwich Hospital map, *c.* 1820.

79 Langley: the buildings as displayed on the notice board at the Stubblick chimney.

80 Langley station bridges. One carried the flue over the railway.

were important. For the rest the basics included grain to make 'crowdy' or bread. An interesting difference in the diet of coal miners and lead workers is that the former tended to eat better. There is also a curious fact that adult lead miners were not so hungry, although their children were. This must have been related to the conditions in which they worked.

Their children were educated after a fashion; some of the mining companies were philanthropic and did not neglect their employees. Literacy levels among lead miners were high. As the industry became more technical and efficient, control over the workforce became stronger to such an extent that the Quaker London Lead Company could insist on temperance, encourage the growth of chapels and churches and even fine people for swearing. Fathers of illegitimate children could be pressurised to marry the mother. The bottom line was the threat of dismissal in an area where there was no alternative work.

In writing a tour of Northumberland and the Border, published in 1859, Walter White has some interesting observations to make at Nenthead about morality. We sometimes assume that Victorians expelled women who had illegitimate babies (trembling music, the father pointing to his daughter and baby the way into the deep snow, with 'Go, and never darken my doorstep again', etc.) but Walter, from the South of England, was very impressed by the way it was handled in the mining areas. He writes this:

> You will not hear of actions for divorce, or of the criminal causes whence such actions proceed; but you will hear of one offence against good morals, and that is, bastardy. If there were such an instrument as a moralometer, you would find bastardy to be a pretty steady high reading in the mining districts. We must not, however, suffer ourselves to be misled, though we may be surprised by such a state of things. It does not necessarily follow that there is more wickedness in these villages than in towns, which, by comparison, show a smaller return of illegitimate births... For here, in this lead-mining country, a girl does not lose caste by having borne a child out of wedlock; though trouble may be occasioned at first, she continues to live in her father's house, sharing still the privileges of home, and is not despised by her mother and sisters. Neither is her chance of marriage diminished, though not as a matter of course with her first lover; and once married, she becomes a faithful wife, and a mother of a hardworking family, is there to participate in all the ameliorating influences which time and circumstances may bring. But should she play the wanton, and repeat the offence, then she forfeits her position and prospect of matrimony.

He goes further, and says that as far as morality is concerned, 'the lead-mining areas stand out in bright relief compared with those in the Durham coalfield'. There is an interesting experience that he describes when he walked to Allendale and was refused accommodation everywhere he tried. The same thing happened at Catton. The explanation came later to him, after he had formed a very poor opinion of local people: apparently he might have been mistaken for one of Her Majesty's Corps of Engineers, who were engaged on the Ordnance Survey of Northumberland and who had 'won a reputation for gallantry as well as trigonometry, and here and there an increase of population takes place in a way not recognised as lawful by the Registrar-General'. He thought it didn't say much for Northumbrian discernment that he should have been mistaken for one of them. He does not complain about the state of his feet after all that enforced walking, however.

Some settlements such as Allenheads were built specifically around mines and smelt mills, so workers did not have far to travel. Because seams could become less productive or the price of lead fall, there had to be some movement from mine to mine, some flexibility, and this was made possible by a system of lodging houses (known as 'shops'). People couldn't jump in to their 4x4s and drive to work; they walked. If work was too far away for a day return, they took their week's supply of food on a Monday morning and stayed in a crowded lodging house, usually sleeping two to a bed with all the windows closed, in an atmosphere that could spread lung disease. The food that they took with them was usually bacon, bread and potatoes. As milk did not keep for long, tea was the favoured drink, especially as alcohol was forbidden. This contrasted with the hard drinking of many coal miners.

Some might find accommodation in other houses. If the lodging were 'temperance', they would not be allowed alcohol, which led to some stability. On Friday nights they returned to their homes for the weekend, and most went to chapel on Sunday. There might be lending libraries for children and adults provided by the companies, who considered worker welfare important for mixed reasons, not necessarily altruistic. They could not afford to lose their workforce. Good workers were good money, and this too depended on how contented they were. And what was the life expectancy of one of these miners? About forty-five years.

Statistics on the death of miners in Allenheads show that from January 1813 to April 1841 this was the pattern of deaths of miners:

15-20 years (11); 20-30 (32); 30-40(12); 40-50 (35); 50-60 (34); 60-70 (49); 70-80 (26); 80-90 (13).

The average life of miners in this area was forty-eight years for men and fifty-three years for women over a period of twenty years.

In twenty-eight years there were 212 deaths, whose average age was fifty-one years and six months. Serious accidents were rare. 'The only disease, to which lead ore miners are especially subject, is provincially called 'being broken-winded' or chronic asthma, or chronic bronchitis, and which generally terminates in phthisis pulmonalis.'

Their lives were based on supply and demand for lead, with no leeway for 'diversification'. Lead miners, as opposed to smelters, were strongly bound to the country where they lived, and preferred to weather out recession rather than move.

There were many fluctuations, and the companies tried to keep their workers in time of recession, knowing that without them the industry might not recover. Men could earn more money in coal mining, but once their homes were established in the fresh air, they preferred to stay where they were. Disease ate out their lungs. Dust was the hazard, caused especially by underground blasting. Charges would be laid, and one man was left to set them off. If there were no adequate ventilation, the dust would linger. Theoretically they should have waited for this to clear, but time was money. Small slivers of minerals reached the lungs and scarred them, opening them up to infections such as tuberculosis (not recognised at the time). The men complained of shortage of breath and coughed up black phlegm. There must have been many who spent their last years in breathlessness and coughing.

Fumes from smelt mills killed vegetation and animals – a reason for carrying them as far away as possible by flues. The acrid smell was intolerable. One wonders what happened to the lungs of children who went through the flues to scrape off any accumulated lead from the walls.

When a man died the wife and children went on living in the same house, and as soon as possible the children would go to work. There was some parish relief offered by the companies. When the mines finally had to close, the only option for the family was to leave the area, some migrating to places like Australia, others finding work in coal and related industries.

There were labour problems. Companies may have considered it prudent to care for the welfare of their workers; there were owners and agents who were concerned for people rather than their profits, but disputes broke out. Generally, the companies tightened their control over labour as time went on. The worst result of dispute was when 'scab' labour was brought in. That brings the narrative to one of the bitterest pieces of invective in the annals of mining. It was the result of a dispute at Allenheads in 1849. The industry was running quite well, but Thomas Sopwith, a man of great ability but overbearing in nature, wanted to modernise in a way that threatened what miners saw as their traditional freedoms. A time clause had been added to contracts, a kind of clocking-in system, which they regarded as spying. In a letter to the *Newcastle Guardian* Sopwith wrote, 'I consider the minds of the great bulk of the Allenheads miners to be inflamed by the ignorant and malicious conduct of a few demagogues', whom he sacked.

Things grew worse, with constables brought in with staff, pistols and handcuffs to support the 'watching' system (spying) to ensure that the miners worked 8 and not 7 hours a day, as Sopwith would have it. Then Sopwith left the problem in the hands of another. It was a no-win situation for the miners, because it wasn't harming the Beaumont concerns very much and other miners were working to that system. At Swinhope Primitive Methodist chapel one of the strike leaders spoke against the blacklegs who would break the strike. He began with a trick of Mark Anthony's in *Julius Caesar* by withholding an important document. Mark Anthony had withheld for politic reasons Caesar's will, which he later revealed made the people his heirs. The workers' demagogue in this case says:

I have a letter in my pocket which I am not prepared at present to let you all see or else you would all take courage anew and cry with one voice 'the day is ours' (putting his hand into a pocket and pulling out a letter but did not).

Now lads, my orders out of this pulpit to this meeting is that every man has liberty to begin work, but it is my hope and earnest prayer that if any man do begin work in connection with them that has begun, that you will have the goodness to pass by them and their wives and families without speaking to them, to have no connexion or communication with them. If they be sick do not visit them; if they are in need of a doctor do not seek them one; if they die do not bury them; if they are fastened underground in the mines do not assist them in seeking them out but let them die, or be killed in the dark, and go from darkness to darkness into the fangs of the devil, to be kept by him without remorse in the fire of hell for ever and ever.

You are all to torment them while on earth, and when they die may the devil take them all to eternity. Let them be like Cain, deserted by God and forsaken of men. Let them be like Judas, only fit for taking their own lives if none of you do it for them... and if they emigrate to Australia or America, if any of you should be there, be sure to treat them in the same way; for I can tell you for one that if I had a houseful of bread and every other necessary of life to take and to spare I would not give one of them a mouthful to save their lives if I saw them dying of want in scores and I hope you will follow my example.

This speech is thought to be by Joseph Heslop. Whoever made it, his reading of the Bible bears all the vindictiveness of the Old Testament and nothing of the compassion of the New. The parody on Christ's teaching is frightening! It is supposed that a copy of this was made by someone at the meeting and handed over to the mining agent. The strike lasted four months in an industry that was relatively free from them. About 100 miners lost their jobs, including the leaders, and most emigrated. Sixty men, women and children went to America on 17 May 1849. (Dickinson, 1903, quoted in Hunt, 1970, *The Lead Miners of the Northern Pennines.*)

One can understand the anger against those who break strikes. Cornish tin miners were sometimes brought in, and lead miners themselves went in 1831-32 to break a North-Eastern coal strike.

Thomas Sopwith had certainly become an object of venomous attack over his proposed reforms to make the industry more efficient, but a year before this strike Allenheads Library had been established 'for the use of the miners, etc, in the employment of T. WENTWORTH BEAUMONT, ESQ. and for the agents and other inhabitants of the upper part of EAST ALLENDALE, subscribing thereto in conformity to the rules.'

This was signed by Sopwith. Members of the Improvement Society paid 6d a quarter, other workers paid 1 shilling, and agents and clerks of the mining office paid 2 shillings.

A Children's Library was established in 1850 'for the use of those Subscribers to the Library who have families'. The books on loan were for 'amusement and instruction'.

As far as we know, the lack of industrial dispute was partly a result of some care for the welfare of workers and their families. So what kind of life was it for children? There is some information in *Evidence on the Employment of Children in 1841*, a government enquiry similar to that into the condition of towns described in this book.

We learn that children worked ore, except one or two who attended trapdoors in the mines. No women were allowed to work in or about the mines. Children who washed the ore were rarely below ten years old, and persons working underground were rarely below eighteen. Adults worked generally no more than a six-hour day for five days a week according to this report, although this was not the case for many.

> Boys work from 7 to 7, exclusive of one hour and a half for meals. Corporal punishment is forbidden and never administered. Discharge is the greatest punishment. There is an excellent school here in which the miners' children are taught for ½d a quarter; there is also a reading room and a lending library.

Children seldom worked in the winter working ore. A thirteen-year-old, Thomas Ashman, is described thus:

> he reads (fairly), writes his name (badly), goes to a Wesleyan school often, and to chapel there. Father is dead, was a lead miner. Was 3 days bad this summer, and off work, with a cold. Works in the open air always.

Anthony Johnson, sixteen, 'had been working for six summers. He sieved refuse for two years, and since then has been lead washing.' It records that he had worked on occasions until midnight in the period from April to October, after which work ceased because the frost laid them off. If the weather is good in the winter, washing continues. He has worked for two winters "getting ore" when it is frosty. In 1840 he had 225 shifts at working (ore) bouse including overtime.

The report says that the boys are 'generally well fed'. It adds that 'some families may be in great debt, and this may make some difference in the feeding. In winter boys are generally better clothed. Boys get a fair schooling. No boys go to any night-school.'

There were other centres of the lead industry, not all on such a large scale as this. For example, the Langley Barony Mines near Haydon Bridge were active only from 1873 to 1893, yet have left a strong but overgrown presence: the engine and crushing houses, dressing floors including some fine circular buddles, and piles of waste. Susan Hartley has researched this neglected part of the story in her accessible booklet, *In the Bewick Vein* (Hartley 1999).

81 The Joicey Shaft area.

Haydon Bridge is where the artist John Martin was born. William Feaver (Feaver 1975) says that at the time of Martin's birth:

> It was easy to envisage lead-mines as the mouths of infernal regions, nearby Hadrian's Wall and border towers as the relics of vainglorious powers. Martin, the artist of flood, apocalypse and disordered time-scales, could not have been born at a more appropriate time or in a more formative place.

Five of his brothers and sisters survived infancy; their mother prophesied that the brothers would make their mark in history. They all seemed to have some sort of genius. One was to misuse it by setting fire to York Minster as a rebellion against the 'whited sepulchres' of the Established Church! The proximity to John of the Tyne Valley, Roman ruins, and particularly the Allen gorge are seen as great influences on his re-creation of the world of Moses, Joshua and Satan. As Feaver says:

> He used to get up at 2 o'clock in the morning and stand in the dark waiting to see the miners' lamps bobbing along the horizontal dark tunnels. He mentions the terror of the open pits, how once, as they played blindfolded, his sister saved him from folly. It was a landscape of extremes that became a theme for his work. Perhaps we can see through him the mining area as hell.

Another artist in another time is W.H. Auden, upon whom the region was to exercise its power (1999 Myers, M. *et al.*). His favourite area was Alston Moor, of which he writes in 1924:

> The smelting-mill stack is crumbling, no smoke is alive there.
> Down in the valley the furnace no lead-ore of worth burns;
> Now tombs of decaying industries, not to strive here
> Many more earth-turns.

As the authors of this booklet point out, the following lines appear in *New Year Letter* (1940), linking the North Pennines into a whole for him:

> I see the nature of my kind
> As a locality I love,
> Those limestone moors that stretch from Brough
> To Hexham and the Roman Wall,
> There is my symbol of us all....
> Always my boy of wish returns
> To those peat-stained deserted burns
> That feed the Wear and Tyne and Tees,
> And, turning states to strata, sees
> How basalt long oppressed broke out
> In wild revolt at Cauldron Snout...
>
> The derelict lead-mining mill,
> Flued to its chimneys up the hill,
> That smokes no answer any more
> But points, a landmark on Bolt's Law
> The finger of all questions. There
> In Rookhope I was first aware
> Of self and not-self, Death and Dread...
>
> There I dropped pebbles, listened, heard
> The reservoir of darkness stirred.

There is one site of a smelt mill where some of the remains seem to have been 'landscaped' to fit the whim of a landowner. What is left of the Dukesfield site in Hexhamshire (near Whitley Chapel) lies just inside a wood on a public footpath. It was in production in 1625 and closed down in 1835. It was used for smelting ores from Allendale and Weardale and in 1811 had roasting furnaces, ore hearths, slag hearths and a refining furnace for the extraction of silver.

What is preserved today is rather difficult to understand. At first it appears as two fine gothic arches of ecclesiastical proportions, built of stone and lined with brick. Above these arches is a flat bridge. It would seem that the ore was roasted under arches. The 'pigs' of lead produced would have been taken away by pony for eventual shipment to Blaydon Mills for use as roofing and pipes. It was a Beaumont-Blackett enterprise.

There is a possibility that the 'bridge' carried a flue from the smelter to a chimney, but this is not clear from the site today. What remains, along with the walling on either side of the burn and signs of weirs and dams, is dramatic and beautiful.

So far, the focus has been on the lead industry, what remains of it, and part of its story. There is much more. The North East has high-quality coal seams, and there has been widespread extraction, not just on the coastal areas.

The end of such collieries, including that at Ford Moss (Beckensall 2001), depended on how far they were from navigable water or from waggonways and railways to carry the coal. All over the county in the sedimentary rock areas are bell pits – circular shafts with a collar around them, too numerous to list here. Often they appear today as green mounds where the land has been disturbed

82 Dukesfield smelter (old print).

83 Dukesfield smelter today.

and a richer growth of grass follows. There were no collieries on the scale of the coastal ones. Mines like that at Plashetts, near Kielder, could not compete despite access to a railway. Plashetts colliery was helped by the construction of roads and bridges. Falstone has a good example of a bridge built by Sir John Swinburne in 1843 at his own expense, to carry the toll road to Scotland. The colliery proved more profitable than other local ventures, and led to their closure. People had used it for domestic supplies for many years, but by 1870 it produced 400 tonnes a day, much of it used for coke. By 1911 one could see coal workings, coke ovens, limekilns, workshops and waggonways. The coal company collapsed in 1926 after the pit had flooded during the Miners' Strike. Eventually it was drowned in the Kielder reservoir. Relics of the old Border Counties railway, begun at Hexham in 1855 and opened at Redesmouth in 1860, had stations at Falstone and Kielder two years later on its route to Riccarton and the link with Scotland. By 1960 the track had been lifted, but parts of the route are visible, as are such bridges as that at Falstone and – a superb feat of engineering – the skew arches and castellated parapet of the Kielder viaduct.

Stone quarries are abundant, many abandoned when housing materials shifted from stone to brick, mostly a by-product of the clays from coal-mining areas. Sandstones of varied quality are available for building a range of domestic, industrial and defensive sites. Builders of structures such as Hadrian's Wall scooped out rock along its course and the shadows of these hollows are visible, especially in low light. Road building made use especially of whinstone, and Cawfields car park is built on a huge quarry, with the face of cut whinstone leaving the Roman wall high in the air and a deep pond.

The process goes on today as the demands of road building intensify. Special stone such as that from Harden continues to be popular for coloured gravel, and the sand and gravel-working companies continue to look for more opportunities. At Caistron, near Rothbury, the extractions have been turned into a lake with islands and bird sanctuary, and a new proposal near Humshaugh is offering attractive lakes to follow similar extraction when the proposals are agreed.

Some of the most attractive ruins are of limekilns, found everywhere. They vary from the church-like structure at Holy Island with its connecting waggonways (Beckensall, 2001), part of a string of coastal kilns that include Seahouses and Beadnell, to many inland and often hidden ones. They are all fascinating. Some have been well preserved, such as those near to Housesteads and the kiln at Great Tosson, near Rothbury, designed by the architect George Reavell of Alnwick, but all speak of a departed era when lime for fertiliser, cement, painting and cleansing was produced locally before crushing machinery made them all redundant. The heyday of the limekiln was from 1750 to 1900, although there are earlier examples.

There is a remarkable building on the A68 that looks at first to be some sort of castle, but is in fact an iron-smelter. In the same area is what looks like clusters of

84 The Cawfields quarry that destroyed part of the Roman wall.

85 *Above and below* Lime kilns in various states of preservation at Housesteads and Ryal.

86 Ridsdale ironworks.

eggs: rounded piles of waste thrown up from iron-ore extraction. This is a famous site as it provided the iron for Armstrong's revolutionary breach-loading gun, and his armaments were tested there. All were linked to Newcastle by rail.

At Hareshaw Lynn, near Bellingham, is a lovely valley with a waterfall; that, too, has an industrial history. It was the availability of local coal to fuel the blowing engines that were to replace waterpower that made ironworking possible. Further south, there was ironworking in the Wark area from the fourteenth-century bloomeries – based on mounds of charcoal and ironstone, which were heated sufficiently to extract the iron for purely local production. At Hareshaw the iron came from nodules that were embedded in shale over 8m thick on land owned by the Duke of Northumberland. Production began in 1838, with two blast furnaces followed quickly by a third, water and steam power providing the blast. There were collieries at Hareshaw and a railway linked smelters with the coalfield. Coke was made on the spot. The operation ran at a loss, as the ore was difficult to access, with transport and markets far away. It shut down in 1848, having housed eighty workers and their families in terraces. An operation of this kind has left its mark on the land, as there were twenty-four kilns for roasting ore, three limekilns and engine sheds for four engines. There were carpenters' shops and a blacksmiths. Elsewhere the scars of extraction remain.

Other sites were at Haltwhistle and Brinkburn. In the latter case, there are still the remains of a circular hearth; the furnace burst open during firing and a huge mass of iron-rich slag lies there. To the north, on the road to Longframlington, the fields on either side of the road still bear traces of coal, ironstone and limestone extraction. Brinkburn even had its own little railway station. These traces of an industrial past go largely unnoticed today; the priory is of much more interest to visitors. It is also so easy not to notice that above the priory next to the car park is the rampart and ditch of an Iron Age enclosure of pre-Roman times.

Coal mining was more profitable in the North Tyne Valley; perhaps it had been going on in the seventeenth century with small-scale 'addit' mines and bellpits. Some coal was needed to burn limestone, and a pit was sunk at Kielder in 1787 for this. The coal extraction at Hareshaw, which fed the iron industry, was soon exhausted and indicates the problems of making large investment in such areas.

These are relatively small-scale industries, but traces of even the biggest have almost disappeared. The great iron and engine works at Bedlington on the banks of the river Blythe was in operation from the 1730s to the 1860s. The motto of the workers was: We Live by Fire, Water, Iron and the Grace of God. This became one of the most important centres of industry in Britain, and it was not just the locally available materials that kick-started the industry, but great inventions that sustained and developed it. Its products ranged from nails to locomotives and railway lines. Water surged through the leets and channels from the river to power the bellows of the hearths and hammers. In the eighteenth century it had the only blast furnace in Northumberland, but this was abandoned and the works concentrated on rolling iron. This proved crucial to the development of railways in 1819 when Michael Birkenshaw produced lengths of malleable iron rails. The Stockton & Darlington Railway trains ran on them. William James announced to the Liverpool & Manchester Railway Company in 1821:

> Light has at length shone from the North and I pronounce it as my candid opinion that the malleable iron rail-road at Bedlington works is by far the best that I have ever seen.

They adopted it to construct that railway. Not content with that success, the owner went into production of locomotives. So successful was it that over 150 were built and exported as far as Persia. One engine, the *De Arend* ('*The Eagle*') was exported to Holland in 1839 and became the first steam engine there.

So what remains of this vast enterprise? The ironworks closed in 1867 and the site was abandoned. It must have been very eerie to wander among the ruins of the crumbling giants. Some buildings have survived within living memory and, although the main site was landscaped into a park (Dene Park) in the 1950s, some structures survive and there are deposits lying beneath the surface. Lost structures are being recovered by resistivity surveys. Local schools have been recruited to help with this recording of what remains, especially the furnace bridge, a kiln and riverside walls.

Attitudes to the past differ so much from generation to generation. Since the Second World War we have flattened and buried so much of what we now regard

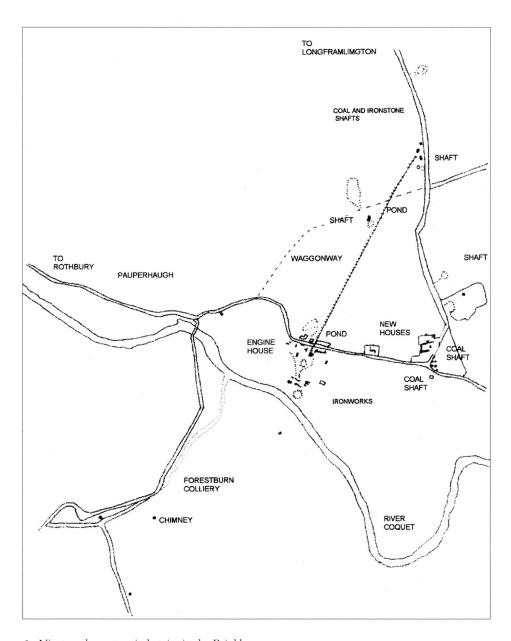

87 Nineteenth-century industries in the Brinkburn area.

88 Bedlington ironworks in 1827.

as irretrievably valuable, and are afflicted with a stultifying sameness in design, especially in towns. This makes it even more important not to lose more of our heritage, which still exists in remote corners of the county, speaking of a past that has given rise to us. It is not too late to resurrect parts of the past, to preserve and display it. The future will not thank us if we do not.

What is so poignant about Northumberland and Tyneside is that so much enterprise has been thrown away or lost, and little has taken its place. I am not impressed with the proliferation of service industries, and the whole metro shopping complex fills me with horror. Who produces the goods that are sold there? Where is the local manufacturing base that was once the envy of the world? Forget Armstrong's guns, which led to the mass slaughter of the First World War, that incredible power struggle fuelled by royal ambitions and incompetent generals. Why did we lose our lead in railway technology? Why have our privatised railways changed from being the greatest in the world to the incompetent and dangerous jumble that they now are?

Why should countries such as France and Italy, to whom we exported our products, now be able to run clean and efficient rail services, while ours get worse? Where are the manufacturing centres that will bring back our lead? Why do we as taxpayers continue to fund incompetent directors and to support sub-contractors that seem more concerned with profits and returns to stockholders than with efficiency, economy, comfort and safety?

The price of the loss of significant industry has been unemployment and the break-up of traditional communities. We must not, however, look to a golden past, because it was sheer hell for some people, with overwork, accidents and early death only too common. Industry came with a price. They were not the 'Good Old Days' – a phrase used because of the belief that what can't hurt us anymore must be better than now. There are plenty of examples in this book of what life was like for many people, but having just looked briefly at the success and decline of the Bedlington iron industry, a victim of developments in other towns such as Middlesbrough, we might consider this report of 1842 by the Children's Employment Commission on Jeremiah Davidson, who was employed at the ironworks:

> Aged 13. Is now at the rolling mill. Comes at a little before 6am and goes away at from 5 to 6, or sometimes 7 o'clock. The heat sometimes makes his head ache and makes him sweat many times. Never was struck but once, 5 or 6 months since, when one of the men struck him over the legs with a pair of tongs; never told anybody. About three times has been laid off parts of days from having his head bad from over-heat; the doctor gave him some stuff to throw up. Can read (fairly); write his name; went to school at the Iron Works School for 2 or 3 years. Goes to Sunday school, and to chapel afterwards.

Just a little glimpse into one life. Multiply that by thousands of other reports on those who otherwise get no mention in history, and we might arrive at a clearer picture of the past.

To conclude this section we take a look at smaller industries that have left traces in the landscape.

In agricultural centres like Hexham, the availability of so many animals and a demand for leather and other skins provided extensive employment for many in their own homes – a cottage industry when it came to sewing skins together to produce the famous gloves called 'Hexham tans'. I have written about this elsewhere (Beckensall, 2001) and indicated where there are many visible remains of the tanning and woollen industries.

Further along the Tyne to the west is Haughton Mill, about 600m from the castle, a partly demolished building that was a paper mill founded in 1788. Its function is given away by the slatted wooden openings, part of the drying shed. This attractive and well-preserved building has an interesting claim to fame: when the French Revolution had formed its government there was a plot in England to undermine its currency by flooding the French market with forged Assignats.

Established in 1793, a paper mill at Fourstones is still working in nineteenth-century buildings, housing the country's oldest Fourdrinier papermaking machine.

Availability of local clay allowed rural brickworks and tileworks to develop, though these had by the twentieth century generally died out in favour of bigger enterprises in the South East. One exception is the Swarland Brickworks, which is still exploiting a depth of glacial clay to the east of Thrunton Forest, just off the A69 past the Newmoor crossroads.

89 Haughton paper mill.

90 Swarland Brickworks in the 1970s.

91 Opencast coal extraction near Acklington (Butterwell)

Estates like Ford, Capheaton and Dilston had their local works, traces of which remain. As the agrarian revolution sped up there was a great demand for drainage pipes too, and these were essential in the improvement of drainage within towns. To illustrate the number of bricks needed in the county, the only remaining glass cone in the whole area at Lemmington was made of about 1¾ million bricks!

Clay was needed for pottery and for firebricks, and there was a large industry at Amble in the late nineteenth century. Salt-glazed sanitary ware was made at Haltwhistle and at Corbridge, which still has a bottle-oven. There is a fireclay works at Bardon Mill producing pottery.

This great, widespread range of industry in Northumberland bears witness to enterprise based on local and wider demands, and the remnants in the landscape are silent witnesses to the way in which the needs of society change and to the finite nature of resources. Whole communities that have lived and worked in these areas have left slight traces of their passing. There are photographs of some, census returns bring out their names, and family history research unearths others, but it is the scars and changes left on the landscape that perhaps leave the strongest impression. It is particularly poignant to find signs of dead communities in areas now partially reclaimed by grasses, shrubs and moorland plants. Shadows form in hollows or emphasise upstanding fragments of industries and homes.

five

Crossing the land

COMMUNICATIONS

Mobility and restlessness have become two main elements in modern life. Roads choked with vehicles taking people to work and school join with the goods carriers; railways carry smaller proportions of traffic each year. Problems of parking have become horrendous and are made even worse as more private cars are bought each day. Yet it is still possible to drive through rural Northumberland without encountering much traffic. In parts there are huge timber transporters to feed the chipboard industry, and military vehicles in the Otterburn area. In summer the rush is on to the seaside or to Scotland. There are still places that are almost empty of traffic. The east coast railway and the Newcastle-Carlisle railway still operate; elsewhere the tribute to branch lines continues through the activities of enthusiastic revivalists.

It is obvious from an OS map that there used to be many small rail links across the county. Now closed down and largely demolished, they are revealed in cuttings, embankments, broken or crumbling bridges and branch station houses with discernible sidings and platforms. There are some superbly engineered viaducts. There are very attractive railway stations that continue in private use, built out of finely quarried freestone blocks. There are twisted (or 'skew') bridges that still carry the ghost tracks over them where they span roads. At Berwick the main line of the railway cuts through a medieval castle; at Ewesley a branch line bisected a circular prehistoric enclosure.

Maps provide an excellent starting point when we seek to understand the different kinds of routes that crossed the land. We also have to look through documents and go out into the field to trace others or confirm what the maps tell us.

There are ghost-roads and tracks, whispering of a change in route. The Devil's Causeway, a feat of Roman engineering, is faintly traceable across moorland north of Longframlington and is resurfaced in other parts. Pony routes are still

92 Ewesley: a railway line bisects a prehistoric earthwork.

93 Ewesley from the south.

94 Ewesley platform and siding today.

95 Newmoor crossroads: modern gas pipeline, stagecoach road and inn, the modern A697 and the buried Devil's Causeway.

visible in the Pennine lead-mining region. Drove roads, hollow ways formed by the passage of thousands of cattle over hundreds of years and by quarry traffic, show up in oblique sunshine. All speak of a change of emphasis in the way that people have used the land and its resources.

This chapter examines some of these traces, a small proportion of what used to be, essential to explorers of our past.

Northumberland is primarily an agricultural county, with 90 per cent still being devoted to farming. On high ground the emphasis is on stock rearing, although there are signs, especially in lynchets, terraces and rig and furrow systems visible in low light, that there was more arable farming at different times in our history. Some of these arable systems go back to a time when temperatures were higher and the growing season longer. These products needed to be taken to market. Almost everywhere there are minerals such as coal, clay, sand, lime, iron, galena and whinstone in variable quantities, not always suitable for large-scale commercial extraction, but of local importance in the past. Traces remain in quarry hollows, bell-pits, limekilns, piles of slag and mining upcast, buildings and in the tracks and roads that served them.

History is about how such resources are used. Pre-Roman society had already established a culture that had changed from a mobile exploitation of food supplies to a more settled life of farming, with the establishment of domestic, defensive and religious centres. By the time the Romans arrived there was a flourishing local culture with its system of communication of trackways and other routes that used dry ridges, linking settlement with settlement. Modern recording ensures that settlements and defences are not seen in isolation; there may be no documents available to trace ancient routes but some may be inferred and some may have been used by subsequent settlers. It is best to forget 'ley lines' as these are imagined rather than real paths across the land. Many features, such as telephone kiosks, can be linked by coincidental straight lines. It is better, for example, to examine real links across areas such as the Milfield Plain, where prehistoric henges and other monuments are linked (Beckensall 2003).

Roman imperial demands were different: a military dictatorship relied for its conquest, expansion and consolidation on swift deployment of men, arms and supplies. Their lines of communication were solidly based, no-nonsense and straight to the point wherever possible. None of your rolling English drunkard roads here. They did not pig-headedly ignore local topography, but drove the roads wherever they could in straight sections, going beyond the wall into Scotland, patrolling the frontier, linking settlements and defences, making trade safe and deployment of troops and materials rapid. Even when buried, such roads may show up from the air. Their quarries are abundantly clear. Their system was a network of major and minor roads, sections of which continued to be used after the Empire collapsed and when they were needed, but they lacked maintenance. It took centuries before Roman technology of major road building was revived. The eighteenth-century road that follows the line of the Roman wall made use of its direction and material. In parts we drive over its foundations, with the wall ditch on one side and the vallum on the other. The Jacobite threat that made it essential to get troops and equipment across country would have been well understood by the Romans.

Roman routes are saved in some place names. The Stanegate, for example, means the stone road, the pre-wall frontier. The Portgate north of Corbridge is the gate through which two major Roman roads north, the Devil's Causeway and Dere Street, made their way towards Berwick and towards the Antonine Wall from Hadrian's Wall. Sections of these major roads can be seen; north of Longframlington at a place called Knogley Gate an excavated section of Dere Street showed a cleared area of 15.24m (50ft) containing ditches 3.05m wide and 0.91m deep (10ft x 3ft), which flanked an 'agger' 7.62m (25ft) wide where the road was built on a foundation of large stones retained by kerbs, then smaller stones of gravel supporting large solid stones as the surface.

The rest of the road can be traced on maps, from the air and by fieldwork. It includes a section from Horton to Lowick that has been metalled over for modern use.

The A68 is on the line of Dere Street for 18 miles north of the wall, mostly on a straight alignment with a roller-coaster course in places, and a journey along this gives a very good indication of the logic of their road building.

96 Portgate. M. Hutchinson

97 The course of the Roman road from West Horton to Lowick.

There are, of course, other Roman ways that are not so well built or spectacular, but there must have been a network for all kinds of local purposes. The work of Ray Selkirk in his aerial and ground pursuit of such routes is a fascinating addition.

A visit to the fort of High Rochester on Dere Street and to the Roman practice camps at Chew Green emphasises the importance of this road, as it runs through bleak, open territory that might have been hostile to Rome. Vindolanda, behind the wall, has Stanegate running past it with an impressive milestone, commonplace at the time. A road linking High Rochester and Learchild, on the Devil's Causeway just north of Edlingham, provides a cross-country link through the Vale of Whittingham, overlooked by the accessible Thrunton Crags.

Whereas the Romans have left such strong traces of their presence, this is not true of many periods in the past. However, the traces are there to be read. In medieval towns communication was essential, as most were market centres. Access to river and sea transport was particularly important if goods were to be 'exported', as trackways soon got bogged down. The maintenance of roads and tracks was usually a local matter, in the hands of landlords, monasteries and parishes, and these may have been reasonably well looked after in parts, but when it came to long-distance routes it was too patchy. Locally the surveyors might be badly paid and labour unwilling. It was possible to travel by stagecoach from Newcastle to Edinburgh by about 1660, and by 1705 180 towns in England had stagecoaches. Part of the Newcastle–Edinburgh route is now bypassed by a more modern road, but it is still easy to explore part of the old road where possible prehistoric east–west routes, the north–south Roman road, the stage road and the turnpike from Rothbury to Alnwick can all be seen in the same area. Add to that the railway at Edlingham to Cornhill and we have a history of local transport.

The most significant change in the concept of road building in more recent times came with the building of turnpike roads; between 1747–1826 they were built on existing roads or along new routes that show as straight lines, made possible by the landlords being able to use unenclosed lands for this purpose, giving easier access to markets and more comfortable surfaces for their coaches. Perhaps for the first time since the Romans used roads and checkpoints to tax people and goods, people had to pay directly for the use of roads at the tollbooths set up for this purpose. The 'Alemouth Road', linking Hexham via Rothbury and Alnwick to Alnmouth, was one of the earliest. Some of its milestones still

98 Edlingham: toll road and railway viaduct cross a more ancient landscape.

hide on the verges. A drive along this long road includes straight and winding sections. At Rothbury the medieval bridge was widened to take it (the two periods can easily be seen from underneath) and a purpose-built bridge was built at Corby's Letch near Edlingham.

In an agricultural area it wasn't built roads that took most of the traffic. Much of the landscape is gouged by deep hollow ways, some of which were used by packhorses (the usual form of carriage before any track was decent enough to take a wheeled vehicle) and some made by generations of animals being driven to markets often hundreds of miles away from north to south, the beasts being fattened on the way. These were 'drove roads', now deep shadowy ruts. It must have been a remarkable experience for the drovers, who would follow routes from Hawick to Falstone and Gilsland, or from Carter Bar to Elishaw and Corbridge or Newcastle. These drovers were highly respected and trusted with all that wealth on the hoof. Not only did they have to drive the beasts safely to market: they had to bring back payment to the owners. Sir Walter Scott paints a picture of the Scottish drovers sleeping rough with the cattle, eating very basic food such as oatmeal. On the route they had to know where to feed the animals; there would be patches of lush grass that the grazing cattle would manure. A village like Elsdon, with hollow ways still visible, has a huge green at its centre that would serve as a stopping place. Money was paid for grazing rights.

The drovers wore distinctive clothes, and had their distinctive mythology and songs. When toll roads were built they would have tried to avoid them. The speed of movement would have been about two miles an hour. They would accept those who wanted to travel with them, for there was safety in numbers in wild areas. Common though they were in some parts of the country, they were still shadowy figures. When it all came to an end with alternative means of transport, I wonder how many young lads were deprived of the chance of travel from Scotland to England with their dogs and horses? It must have been a tough but exciting prospect, and with what stories would they have returned home?

The cattle they brought to market were the Galloways, cattle that were large and that sold well. There were also Kyloes, all shod for the journey. They started out lean, but were fat by the time they were at the market.

Sheep were vitally important to the economy for centuries, but they did not travel so far, and some of the cattle routes that included fords could not be used by sheep. The average journey for pigs was six miles; they were much more difficult to handle.

It is difficult to attribute the use of a routeway to a particular time in history, for a good route is a good route. They follow the line of least resistance, the best drainage, the minimum of hazards. We have hundreds of local routes in footpaths, bridleways and even routes to graveyards that have developed for local convenience. Others, however, were deliberately planned and superimposed on the landscape and on existing older routes. This happened in the age of toll roads, which followed established routes for much of their way. Take, for example, the

99 Elsdon village green, motte and bailey, church and tower. *NUM*

road from Hexham to Alnmouth, known as the Corn Road. The agricultural and industrial revolutions made it essential to get better communications; it was no use producing goods that could not be transported and marketed. The revolutions made it impossible to leave roads in the hands of amateur authorities. At first, though, the payment of tolls was resisted. There is a nice little story from Haydon Bridge in 1771 about John Briddick, the Allendale postman, who was on his usual journey to Hexham on a Galloway pony when he was asked for a toll at the turnpike gate. He is reported to have said it was a shame to demand three-half-pence for his pony, which was no bigger than a dog; and rather than submit to such an imposition, he would take his pony upon his shoulders and walk through with it. This he did, affording the gatekeeper a good laugh!

There had to be a way of creating and maintaining good roads, and a system grew up piecemeal: interested parties could put forward a Bill to Parliament. From 1751-1772 more and more applications were made. The Newcastle-Carlisle Military road began in 1751, paid for by government money but operated as a turnpike. The Corn Road from Hexham was turnpiked in 1752, a necessary step as the demand for more corn intensified. This coincided with the enclosure of more land for arable, a reversal of the policy that had put sheep pasture at a priority, often at the expense of closing villages. By the mid-eighteenth century large areas were enclosed with new walls and hedges, and arable farming was intensified to feed the rapidly growing population. Remaining fields were enclosed, and commons and wasteland were cultivated. The more powerful the landlord, the easier this was, and it was done by an Act of Parliament. We can trace the process on maps. The pattern of rectangular fields with hedges and walls was reflected in the roads, with straight lines and sharp corners at the plough headlands. Look along the route of the Corn Road and see the considerable amount of rig and furrow fields, not of the medieval pattern of wide, S-shaped curves, but of straighter, narrower lines. Follow the road from Hexham to the grain port of Alnmouth, and the contrast between straight, 'modern' sections and the older curves and corners is apparent.

Coach travel increased on the new roads; in Britain turnpikes covered one-fifth of total public highways, with parishes still mainly responsible for them. Wheeled traffic replaced packhorses and sped-up considerably; competition among carriers kept prices down. The early nineteenth century changed the way roads were constructed; it was the age of Telford and McAdam, when there was a graded build-up of road surfaces, the straightening of sections and a reduction of gradients.

With the coming of the railways and the pouring-in of capital and engineering skills to fuel the remarkable enthusiasm that at first greeted them, the turnpikes fell out of favour. It may be difficult for us to appreciate fully the fervour with which people greeted the new age of steam power; there was incredible optimism in Victorian England, a sense of adventure and purpose, an inventiveness that was encouraged to flourish. Fortunes were there to be made (and lost). There were people of the calibre of George Stephenson and Lord Armstrong, who applied their intellect and knowledge to invention, when the North became the trigger to Britain's becoming the Workshop of the World, where people were prepared to take a risk, when progress seemed unending.

To understand what resources were in Northumberland at the time, it is useful to look at the classification of goods adopted by railways. This follows, and is a fairly standard preamble to many reasons put forward for having railways to move such goods:

Manures and road metal.
Coals, lime, ironstone, iron ore and other minerals.

Timber, deals, pitching, pavingstone, coke, culne, charcoal, flags, bricks, tiles, slates, lead, iron and other metals.

Corn, grain, flour, hay and other agricultural produce.

Sugar, dye-woods, groceries, cotton, wool, hides, drugs, manufactured goods.

Other uses of the lines were to be for the transport of passengers and live animals.

All these items were available in Northumberland awaiting transport, and the railway network was designed to open up even remote areas if possible. In return, the shareholders anticipated making their fortunes. Some did, but it was a swings-and-roundabouts situation.

RAILWAYS

In Northumberland the only major railways that remain are the main line east coast route and the Newcastle–Carlisle railway. Part of this narrative concerns itself with those lines that have closed, but it is gratifying that one of the earliest and longest, from Carlisle to Newcastle, still operates. The story has been well told in many publications, but the forerunner of its history was written by Tomlinson in his *North Eastern Railway*, edited in 1967 by Ken Hoole. It is a microcosm of the visions, planning and frustrations of the Railway Age, and a tale worth retelling – at least in part.

The railway, designed to link sea to sea, was a very exciting concept, but not the only one, for an extensive canal system was also proposed. A straightforward plan was devised that involved the removal of only one cottage along its route, not interfering very much with landowners' property, and involving the use of horse-drawn carriages! This would have been quieter and not so objectionable as some steam locomotives.

On 12 November 1825 the first parliamentary notice was given of the main line and seven branch lines. George Stephenson was appointed by Greenwich Hospital to survey the land on the north side of the Tyne, beginning at Warden Bridge near Hexham, heading to the east to Corbridge, then to Thornborough, Heddon and Town Moor, Newcastle. By 1826 proposals were not ready to put to Parliament, so they did not apply that session. In 1828 a line was definitely fixed. Thirty-five landowners objected. Charles Bacon of Styford and his son Charles Bacon Gray were the biggest thorns in the flesh. No matter what the planners did to accommodate them, they objected and on no condition would they allow a railway to go though their property. Others saw that this blocking tactic would not be to their advantage. The position was that there was only one vehicle between Carlisle and Newcastle to carry Newcastle papers and the occasional passenger, two carriers and two stagecoaches that took eight-and-a-half hours to cover the distance. The road was crowded at times and it took three days for other forms of transport. The success of the Stockton-Darlington railway was there for all to see: it was cheap and rapid. The other landlords put pressure on the objectors, although Mr Bacon Gray tried to convince Parliament that his objections were that the best route had not yet been selected. After a fight in Parliament he gave way, eventually picking up the hefty sum of £3,000 in compensation, and the Royal Assent was given to the Bill on 22 May 1829. Thus we had the largest railway sanctioned by Parliament at that time.

In its original form this was very different from what it was to become, for the Bill stated:

> No locomotive or moveable steam engine shall be used on the said railways or tramroads for drawing wagons or other carriages, or for any other purpose whatsoever.

When the concept of traction changed, some landowners were protected from being in sight of any steam engines from their houses, including Charles Bacon of Styford and Nicholas Leadbitter of Warden.

The rail was intended for public use, on the payment of a toll, and a list of goods and prices was laid down.

The company brought in an engineer (Francis Giles) from London to check the route again and report on it; he approved. A very large board of directors was then appointed, and work began in March 1830 at the west between Blenkinsopp and Carlisle when there was still a problem about what to do at the east end. Meanwhile, a terminus was fixed at Blaydon. Economy was an important consideration for these early lines, and in contrast to the superb architecture of so many stations on the later line from Alnwick to Cornhill, on some stations there was no platform. On the Newcastle–Carlisle railway some had a platform on one side only. There were some good stations, of which the large permanent station at Hexham remains an example. Until 1844 the Stocksfield–Hexham line was only a single track; at the Farnley tunnel near Corbridge the single line was doubled.

From this distance contemporary accounts give us so much about the wrangles over routes, about the protection of property, of the sheer effort and expertise – legal, scientific and financial – that went into such enterprises, that it appears like a huge bubbling cauldron from which the product may emerge pure or marred. Shareholders expected to make a fortune, and incompetence of those entrusted with their money could mean ruin. Debates raged in localities through to Parliament. Egos were enhanced and destroyed. What is often neglected is information about the workforce of 'navvies', which was the only means by which it could all happen once decisions about money and routes had been sorted out.

This railway succeeded. On 28 June 1836 the seven-and-a-half-mile stretch from Hexham to Haydon Bridge opened. A procession of two trains started from Blaydon pulled by engines called *Hercules* and *Sampson*. One carriage was occupied by the Allendale band. On 26 July the Hartleyburn and Brampton railway opened as a private colliery line to replace an older waggonway.

The opening of the west portion of the main line was a grand affair, watched by 40,000 people, when a procession of four trains carrying about 400 passengers ran between Newcastle and Greenhead. Somehow the story of official openings has become something like a comedy script, not always funny for those involved. On this occasion the train carrying the mayor and corporation became detached when a coupling gave way. The others had to wait for it for three-quarters of an hour.

That was nothing compared with the opening of the whole stretch of 61 miles on 18 June 1836 (Waterloo Day), when five trains set off from Newcastle for Carlisle. It is best to let the historian of the railways, Tomlinson, tell us the story.

> The Corporation of Carlisle and the directors from the west crossed the river in the barges of the Mayor of Newcastle and the Trinity House, the other visitors in steam packets. This part of the day's proceedings was marred by a regrettable incident. A gangway between the Quay and one of the steam packets gave way and twelve or thirteen of the passengers from the second train, among whom were two ladies in dainty silk dresses, a physician and two surgeons from Carlisle got a ducking in the river, which, fortunately, was not more than three or four feet deep at the time.

From the Close the civic bodies of Newcastle and Carlisle marched in procession by way of Grey Street to the Assembly Rooms, where they breakfasted with the directors. On returning to Redheugh about an hour after the advertised time for starting, they found the carriages occupied. The corporation of Gateshead, by arriving in good time, had secured their seats, but the rest of the reserved carriages had been invaded by the crowd. 'Thus situated', to quote the *Gateshead Observer*, 'the civic authorities were reduced to the necessity of looking for seats, and the chief magistrates of Carlisle and Newcastle were obliged to look for refuge in a pig-cart.'

The eating of food and the drinking of toasts figures largely in rail ceremonies that over-indulgence led to, and so does a lack of punctuality! Anyway, one can imagine the affront to dignity among some officials, but this was to be shared by all.

The procession set off, and fog gave way to rain at Ryton and continued all the way to Brampton. Three-and-a-half-thousand people took part, including the historian John Hodgson, who wrote a little gem for us in a letter to his wife on 19 June after the event:

> I may add that one side of my bag, by lying under the seat on which I had sat, had, for an hour or more, before I remembered it, amused itself with talent as a sponge and drunk up so much of the water that poured from our roof of umbrellas as to make my night things wet

as itself and as dirty as the sheep truck on which we were carried: for you must know that its office was new yesterday: sheep and oxen from it on their way to Newcastle had been in the habit of grazing on the beauties of the Tyne: but now it became a pen of bipeds not hairy enough to cover themselves at once with a sealing by which each defended his own head but powered a precious stream into the cap or down the shoulders of his neighbour!

Thomas Sopwith's diary recorded that it took 3 hours 43 minutes to get from Blaydon to Carlisle, of which only 2 hours 37 minutes were spent travelling. The stops were at Stocksfield, Corbridge, Hexham, Haydon Bridge, Haltwhistle and Milton. The last of the procession of trains arrived at Carlisle an hour after it was timed to leave. The passengers had been cooped up for a long time, so naturally when they arrived at Carlisle 'a disorderly stampede for refreshments took the place of a procession into the town which was to have formed part of the day's proceedings'.

When it was nearing the time to leave:

early comers took possession of the covered carriages, entering the windows when the doors were locked. Several ladies of portly town councillors, with a temporary loss of dignity, secured comfortable seats in this way.

Time had to be allowed for the trains to be prepared for the return journey, so when the trains were supposed to arrive at Redheugh they were still in Carlisle.

'Passengers who had taken their seats at 6.30pm did not get away until nearly ten o'clock, having had to remain for over three hours exposed to the drenching showers in a comfortless station' – presumably with no refreshments and no loos. The ladies had dressed for a summer's day. But that wasn't the end: one train collided with the back of another.

Some carriages and a tender were thrown off the line and two passengers were injured, one having a rib broken and the other a hip dislocated.

So everyone had to sit miles from anywhere surrounded by wild country until 1 a.m., to the great anxiety of those waiting at Redheugh for their return, where 'thousands of people waited all night'. The first train arrived at 3 a.m. and the last at 6 a.m.

This line is still in use, but what about all the other hundreds of miles of track that threaded across the county like veins? The map shows the extent of these branch lines. Some have left spectacular evidence of the engineering skills that went into their making. Viaducts at Kielder and Lambley for example, the former with 'skew' arches, still stand and are awesome. Deep cuttings and long embankments, stations with sidings and engine houses or goods stores, signal boxes, railwaymen's cottages, bridges and the beds of the tracks themselves are

100 Haltwhistle Station today.

101 The water tank at Haltwhistle.

there to be found as fragments in the landscape. Sudden humpback bridges surprise unwary drivers, as the sump grooves on the roads show. I shall offer just a few examples of what survives.

It is possible to find documentary evidence of the establishment and running of these railways and of the engineers responsible for them, but accounts of the lives of the workers who built them are hard to come by. Some are biased and concentrate on the quantities of meat and alcohol consumed by the men and on their reportedly bad morals. Of course they ate and drank a lot: the hard physical labour demanded that the body replaced what it lost. Their work was not confined to one place for long, so they seldom had permanent homes. Known as navvies, after the 'navigators' who built Britain's canals, they had among them many skills, acquired by vast experience. They knew their geology – knowledge that could save their lives. Their main tools were picks and shovels and the extensive use of wheelbarrows. They were not common-or-garden labourers. Life was hard, so what made them take up this job? A simple answer would be money, for they were comparatively well paid in the wage league table. For example, they were paid considerably more than the agricultural worker. Some of these could not feed their families and took to a nomadic way of life

102 The Wanney Line at Ray, near the A68.

looking for work. Many had come from Ireland, driven by famine. Some would be fairly local, but in remote areas the net to recruit them had to be cast wider. They preferred to live in a town rather than in a way-out shantytown, and this put pressure on existing towns. Some of the problems of itinerant labour have been referred to in chapter three. Any pressure on accommodation encouraged the spread of disease, with the existing and often inadequate sanitary structures unable to cope. Few people were concerned about the welfare of the navvy, and would mutter or shout 'good riddance' when they moved on. People in rural areas were frightened of these hard men and the presence of their hard women. As with the behaviour of people in crowded towns, the favourite criticism was reserved for immorality. This example from Bristol in 1832 is typical, in Felix Farley's *Bristol Journal*:

> The character of the Navvies is so well known, that I need scarcely state that swearing, gambling, drunkenness and Sabbath breaking, prevail to a great extent among them. And it would have given me great pleasure to have been able to state, that the last mentioned wicked practice was not observable upon the works.

Railway building was a matter for muscles; Britain did not follow America's example in 1842 and use mechanical excavators. Exceptions were made for the use of steam power in pumping engines for work in tunnels. Building operations have some archives that include drawings, but here is a verbal description by Charles Dickens from *Dombey and Son* in 1846:

> Houses were knocked down; streets broken through and stopped; deep pits and trenches dug in the ground; enormous heaps of earth and clay thrown up; buildings that were undermined and standing, propped by great beams of wood...
>
> Everywhere were bridges that led nowhere; thoroughfares that were wholly impassable; Babel towers of chimneys, wanting half their heights, temporary wooded houses and enclosures, in the most unlikely situations; carcases of rugged tenements, and fragments of unfinished walls and arches, and piles of scaffolding, and wildernesses of bricks, and giant forms of cranes, and tripods straggling above nothing. There were a hundred thousand shapes and substances of incompleteness, wildly mangled out of their places, upside down burrowing in the earth, aspiring in the air, mouldering in the water, and unintelligible as any dream.

This chaos reigned in towns, but the country bore its share of upheaval.

Gunpowder was used in cuttings where there was rock and in tunnel construction, and there were accidents. Elsewhere clay was a misery, as it mingled with water and oozed out over what had been excavated. But it was tunnelling that was most dangerous. Here miners were often brought in to use their vast experience, especially with flooding. Gunpowder was used for blasting, and dynamite later in the century. Tunnels, arches and bridges required timber, so there was an army of carpenters and masons needed. Particular skills were needed to produce the skew bridges, still to be seen at Kielder and Chollerton, so that a track could cross over a road at an angle, when it was easier to build them square and to realign the road. Particularly splendid structures were achieved in the building of viaducts such as that at Lambley over the South Tyne (Colour 19) and many of them in Britain had monumental touches added to them, like the battlemented Kielder viaduct.

Remnants of this work are visible and preserved in Northumberland, but most of what was laid down was the track itself with the laying of sleepers, spiking in the 'chairs' and the rails, and putting down ballast to keep the track firm. Signals, water towers, halts, goods sheds and engine sheds were built. Turntables were needed to turn the trains. The whole thing was a triumph of vision, organisation and skill, but at the cost of many lives and injuries. Techniques remained constant for years, but the new steam hammer was brought in to drive in the piles for the Border Bridge at Berwick. Once the main railways were established, light railways followed.

The destruction of some railways began with the scrapping of track and rails, and these were recycled. Cuttings filled up with self-sown shrubs and trees. Grass and other plants found root on the embankments and tracks. Some bridges were partly demolished for their stone, leaving cross-sections of themselves. Many

103 Detail of the skew construction.

104 *Above* Chollerton skew bridge.

105 *Right* Lambley viaduct.

buildings were taken over and reused, such as the fine stations that became private houses. They exhibit the qualities of design and craftsmanship that made the system the envy of the world. Of particular quality is the Alnwick railway station, that had to fit the status of a ducal town, now partly preserved as Barter Books.

The shadows of the great age of rail, when there was enthusiasm for spreading lines like arteries and veins across the landscape, remain an intriguing and disturbing phenomenon. Partly overgrown, partly destroyed, they can still be experienced and we bring to them a sense of wonder that so much effort and enterprise went into their making. This truly was a revolution, leaving an evocative and uneasy legacy. There may be 'blood upon the coal' behind the coal house door, but there is blood along the railway lines too.

106 Barter Books, a reuse of the Alnwick railway station. *Birtley Aris*

107 Alnmouth Station: unlike Alnwick, this is still in use on the main line. *Birtley Aris*

WHAT REMAINS?

Before selecting some examples of the more visible remains of abandoned railways, it is useful to give a summary of the extent of the rail network.

Names of the companies changed as one group was amalgamated with another, but those in Northumberland included the Newcastle-Carlisle Railway (1829-1862) that, along with the Hexham & Allendale Railway (1865-1876) became part of the North-Eastern Railway (1854-1922), itself becoming the LNER (1923-1947).

Other lines were also amalgamated to form the LNER, including the York, Newcastle & Berwick Railway (1847-1854) and the Blythe & Tyne Railway (1852-1874).

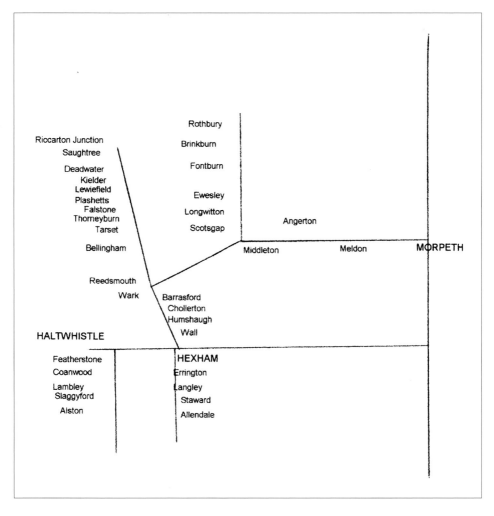

108 Map of the Northumberland railways.

The Border Counties Railway (1854-1860), the Wansbeck Railway (1859-1864) and the Northumberland Central Railway (1863-1872) became the North British Railway (1844-1922) and then part of the LNER.

This information is given to show the complexity of ownership. What follows is an example of what can be seen of some of the lines.

The Wanney Line is well worth exploring, as it runs through some remote and challenging country. It was designed in the 1850s to link Reedsmouth (sometimes spelt Redesmouth) with Morpeth. The plans were drawn up by John Furness Tone, whose family name appears on the Tone Inn on the old Roman road, the A68, before the Sweethope Loch is reached. It was planned for one branch to go through Scots Gap via Rothbury to Coldstream, but it ran out of cash and had to terminate at Rothbury, leaving the route from Alnwick to Cornhill (Coldstream) construction to the North-East Company.

The railway, built by the North British Company, was designed to open up the way to the ironstone deposits at Ridsdale and Broomhaugh. These were focused on Ridsdale and West Woodburn, clearly seen from the A68 – particularly the castle-like remains of the Ridsdale Ironworks and a pub called the Gun, named after the early Armstrong breach-loading gun made of the metal from this area, and the place where subsequent Armstrong armaments were tested. The ironworks, extending to Bellingham, were only short-lived, smelting ceasing in the 1870s, but has left piles of debris and some remains of buildings. In the Woodburn area there are also stone quarries and coal pits. The rest of the land is mainly for sheep and cattle. The railway from Morpeth was thus designed for minerals and the transport of animals, with other traffic for passengers and mail. The cattle market at Scots Gap was an important source of business, and so was passenger traffic during the Bellingham Show and for visitors and troops going to the artillery ranges.

The other branch that went to Rothbury brought coal from Longwitton, Blagdonburn, Forest Burn and The Lee. Lime came from Rothley and from near Fontburn. There was also stone and timber to be transported, and passengers, especially for the Rothbury Races. Perhaps one of the most notable events was when the Prince of Wales and his family arrived at Rothbury station for a visit to Lord Armstrong at Cragside.

Passenger traffic ended in 1952, and by 1958 only the Redesmouth-Bellingham freight service was left, ending in 1963 along with Rothbury.

From Morpeth the trains ran through Meldon, Angerton and Middleton to Scots Gap. Today Scots Gap still has strong reminders of its place as a junction, with a cattle market and the extended Station Hotel building, which is now the headquarters of the National Trust.

A group of North Tynedale teachers, in what they called 'The Tuesday Club', used to meet to discuss matters of environmental and historic interest that could be of use in the school curriculum, and one of their papers published in 1982 was called *The Wanney Line*, by Ian Futers. This outlined the routes, illustrated

109 Track of the Wanney Line at Rothley from Scots Gap.

with sketch maps, with information on what was to be seen, and ended with the results of an appeal through newspapers to people who remembered the line to share their knowledge. One response was from J.R. Lauderdale of Alnwick who had lived at Reedsmouth as a boy. A village of twenty houses, it had a mission hall, a porter's cabin that the local lads were allowed to use in the winter evenings, and even a football team. There was great pride in railway work and a strong sense of community. The engine sheds had no electric light then; tow lamps were used at night when they were cleaning the engines in the sheds. These gave off unpleasant fumes. An interesting comment he makes is about the large number of passengers that got off at 'The Steel' platform, including foreigners, mainly Japanese, on their way to the gun firing. This fits in with the photographs of visitors seen at Cragside.

He remembers the importance of line testing (private companies take note!), where wheeltappers tapped all the wheels of the engines to test for cracks and faults through the note given off.

The sale days were the busiest. He stresses the cleanliness of the wagons and the humane consideration given to animals.

The permanent-way men lived in lonely railway-side cottages and patrolled lines daily – not their only duties, but safety was their priority. It was a great

110 A shed made of sleepers, at Ewesley.

chance for workers to observe nature, and he remembers that rabbits were a problem (as they are today) because they could cause a landslide by burrowing into the embankments. For this reason bushes were planted to hold the soil firm.

Like many other lines, there were many factors that determined where the lines should run and where trains should stop. It was not always a matter of geology either. The Trevelyans of Wallington wanted the railway, but ensured that its route was diverted away from the hall. Ray Halt was a casual halt at the cottages, and was handy for Sir Charles Parsons (of engineering fame) who had a big house nearby (now demolished). The railway at Ray needed to carry snowploughs, as it was high up in places, hence the name Summit Cottages.

One other feature of this railway is that a contractor's branch line was laid down when the Catcleugh reservoir was being constructed. One hut of the workers' accommodation has now been preserved as a museum. A branch up the Broomhaugh Burn led to the artillery testing ground, still a restricted 'danger area'.

six

Rise and fall

Hadrian's Wall is one of the most important ancient monuments in the Western world, reflected by its status as a World Heritage Site. Although it has been denuded by stone robbers for centuries, built into houses, churches and defensive towers and used as the foundations for an east-west road, there is enough remaining material above and below the ground to enable us to piece together some of its history.

Even the parts from which stone has been plucked, sometimes almost entirely, retain sufficient material to trace the wall, its ditch, milecastles, interval towers and its vallum. Shadows particularly pick out the course of the ditches and slight surface traces of buildings. From the air and from the ground the vallum in particular shows up rather like a railway line. (Colour 8)

The wall ditch, built a short distance from the wall to the north, facing enemy territory, was generally V-shaped and deep. The vallum, lying to the south of the wall, was an elaborate piece of quarrying that formed a ditch and low stone-and-earth-dump wall that marked off the military zone, intended perhaps to route travellers through official gaps so that they could be controlled and taxed. Nothing on this scale had been seen before by people living nearby or, for that matter, anywhere else in the Roman Empire. In the central Northumberland section the quarries for its stone are shadow-filled hollows along its length. Quality sandstone was used as an ashlar (outside) facing, and this stone skin held the rubble and clay that gave it body.

Visit any part of the central section, the part that runs from the Portgate, north of Corbridge westward, when the sun is low in the sky, and you will see its remains most vividly. Even the flattened parts of the Corbridge excavated settlement (Coria) behind the wall take on depth and distance. Walls follow the crests and ditches of older ditches. Blocks of masonry lie around like scattered parts of a Lego set in sharp contrast to the manicured lawns. The strongroom

111 General view of Hadrian's Wall.

where standards and pay were kept grows more profound with deepening shadow. Granaries show much more clearly their underfloor spaces where the air could circulate. Marks made by masons, joints, troughs and drains are clear.

One of the most dramatic features of skilled building is at Chesters where the wall crosses the Tyne by a bridge that was based on an elaborate pier. Among the shadow of trees, blocks of stone, so carefully cut, so carefully jointed, reveal themselves in a patterned mosaic. (Colour 8)

At the fort there, inscriptions glow into life: phalli included in walls or on the floor of the headquarters building, signs of a masculine strength, virility symbols that are at home among soldiers, but perhaps there to ward off the evil eye. One phallus was carved on what is now called 'The Written Rock' near to Wall village, at a place where a stone-cutter decided to immortalise himself by writing his name. It was his stone, and he added the phallus for good luck perhaps.

As we see in the Vindolanda writing tablets, any personal information about who was there and what they did gives us a much more human view of those who lived in this area for so long. A close examination of Roman stone speaks also of recycling and a change in function of the wall, which was static in its course but not a one-off building. Like so much else in history, it is subject to decay, change, re-use.

The 'shadow' of the wall provides a metaphor. It must have meant many things to many people over the centuries. Perhaps to those who were around during

112 Vallum at Haltonchesters.

113 Strongroom, Chesters.

114 Chesters bridge foundation, south bank.

115 The Written Rock, recording that it was Carantini's. A phallus is added.

its first construction it was a symbol of their submission and bondage; to others at the same time it may have been a welcome opportunity to make money out of these comparatively wealthy foreigners who were there to stay. They might have stared in wonder at the uniforms and extraordinary discipline of these men of iron, wondered at the colour of their skin and hair, at their different voices. Did they lock up their sons and daughters? Did they decide to go elsewhere to live in peace, only to find the army on the move again behind them? We must not underestimate the survival instinct. Much of Northumberland outside the wall zone was agricultural; the Roman army needed grain and not all of it had to be imported through ports or along the roads. The coastal strip, valleys and the Cheviot Hills were grain producers. There were animals to be hunted for food and skins, and domestic animals to be traded. Eventually the forts along the wall were to accommodate such traders, to incorporate families, and there would be inter-marriage. The so-called Roman army was polyglot anyway; it left traces of its ancestors from regions well beyond Britain, for the Empire was all-absorbing.

In another sense the wall has cast a shadow on the archaeology of other periods, for the Classics have been so deeply rooted in our educational system that there was an opportunity to meet Rome second-hand. Roman remains are incredibly durable and incredibly rich when compared to some of the traces of our prehistoric ancestors. For me, a single day's excavation at Vindolanda produced more finds than could be made in weeks of excavating some upland prehistoric site.

The interest generated by the wall has also poured funding into its excavation, not only from the common purse, but also from rich individuals who could even afford to buy a whole stretch of wall to prevent its being quarried for building stone.

Today it is big business, for it attracts thousands of visitors from all over the world. It also continues to surprise in the richness of its finds and in the ever-changing interpretations of its history and purpose. It's something to which the public can relate: all those shoes, cooking pots, tools, jewellery, altars and fabrics, all in a setting that lends itself to intelligent reconstruction.

The wall zone has other delights. Because the central section follows the rise and fall of fault lines with ridges of sedimentary rock and the dramatic upheaval of whinstone, it is a superb centre for walking, looking, painting and taking photographs. This is in all weathers too. Now it is possible to walk its length.

RECYCLING THE PAST: DECLINE, FALL AND REBUILDING

Just as the wall has provided material for farms and other buildings along its length, it has contributed to many of our more famous buildings. The crypt of Hexham Priory made use of many robbed stones, probably from the Roman

116 Excavation at Vindolanda: Andrew Birley discusses a find with a young archaeologist.

117 Out of the mud, a Roman brooch.

118 General picture of the wall zone.

119 Ermine Street Guard: shadows made flesh.

settlement at Coria. Throughout the building are other fragments, including the massive, impressive memorial to Flavinus, altar stones, inscriptions, Roman gods and decorative pieces.

Studies of any old building do well to concentrate on changes in the fabric, for these provide a comment on what was valued and why. For a structure to become a convenient quarry was hardly a token of respect, yet it was a shortcut for the later builders and might even supply the technology that they found difficult to imitate or better.

Corbridge church, built on the same terrace as the Roman settlement but further to the east, has used an arch of the headquarters building as the mainstay of its Saxon tower. The exterior west wall of this tower is a delight for those who enjoy visually such changes in style and use. The picture illustrates this very clearly.

At Chollerton church, Roman pillars have been brought in from one of the forts to provide an aisle.

On a different scale, there is a garden at Corbridge sloping down to the river where the owner discovered all sorts of interesting pieces of stone sculpture, illustrated here. The garden wall already had a segment of volcanic quernstone

120 Corbridge church tower, west.

imported from Germany (as many others were) embedded with part of an altar and various pieces from a medieval church. The heads that he discovered in the soils and small pieces of pillar provide fragments of the Corbridge story over a big span of time.

As we have seen, a Saxon gravestone at Warden was made from a reused Roman monument. St John Lee vicarage garden uses a Roman altar as a sundial. All this is understandable, given the ease with which such stones could

121 Above and next page Multi-period finds from a Corbridge village garden.

be pillaged. It took a change of attitude to regard the past as something to be preserved as close as possible to its original state, and before we deplore what happened to so much Roman building, spare a thought for the recent vandalism that has turned parts of our cities into uniform featureless deserts at the expense of what we might regard as fine architecture. There has always been a strong element that has thought the past to be irrelevant, to be swept aside, to make way for something more profitable. Not many years ago in Alnwick there were people who seriously advocated the destruction of the Hotspur Tower to make the flow of traffic easier. There is nothing new about this: it is difficult to think that some people in ancient Egypt, even those in charge of tomb-building, should have been organising the systematic plunder of older tombs for their own profit, without fear and without respect.

The best way to preserve old buildings is to use them; some of the redundant railway stations of the post-Beeching age have a new life as homes, shops, or restaurants. Large halls in which no one wants to live become hotels, offices and conference centres. Langley station has become a garden centre. The track leads as a green way under two bridges, one that carried the smelter flue-tunnel over the railway line, with a twisted arch, and there is a walk to the reservoir, now a haven for water birds.

There is another aspect to recycling. A form of architecture may become unfashionable. This affected churches, and shows in the change from Norman to Gothic, to Perpendicular, to Victorian. Images were smashed because they were periodically deemed heretical. Out went the work of skilled carpenters, masons and stained glass artists.

Changes in population could make whole buildings or parts of them redundant. The church at Alnham, tucked away in what is now a backwater, once served a much bigger congregation. The filling-in of the arches of the north nave after the removal of an aisle was a sure sign that the population had shrunk.

Churches show these trends, not only in population but also in wealth. Their ownership by a person of wealth and standing would make all the difference to the quality of building and its decoration. The landed gentry would cover walls with their family memorials and armorials. Although Northumberland does not have the sad spectacle of totally isolated and redundant churches as we see in Norfolk, it does have buildings that have remained as population dropped. Throckrington St Aidan's is one such church, where the earthworks of homes abandoned in the early nineteenth century are visible as shadows in low light. Some villages closed down, and have left only outlines in the ground.

Whereas this solitary church with its Norman foundation is isolated today, there are faint earthworks around it where a village stood. They were rectangular and had garths (yards), especially to the north. There were eighteen taxpayers in 1296 and in 1666 eleven houses were listed for Hearth Tax. It is said that imported disease destroyed the population.

Depopulation by disease caused the abandonment of Ancroft village, where it wiped out so many families. Once housing a flourishing community, there is a

122 Throckrington church on high.

large field lined to the south with trees, reputedly planted for each family that suffered loss. The roads and house sites are clear, especially in low light. The dead were carried to a field to the south-east of the church and burnt there.

Other villages suffered depopulation when landowners chose pasture to replace arable farming, thus reducing the need for so many workers on the land. One spectacular abandoned settlement is at South Middleton on the south bank of the river Wansbeck on both sides of the Bolam–Scots Gap road. Crofts run from east to west overlooking a village green, which was later encroached on by rig and furrow-ploughing for arable. There were twelve taxpayers in 1296, and people were still living there in 1635.

The area around Bolam is covered with rig and furrow, preserved because arable farming was largely abandoned. The fine churches in that area, some featured in this book, show that there was some wealth and a fairly substantial population.

123 Middleton South deserted village in the snow: houses and fields. *NUM*

West Whelpington was excavated in advance of quarrying. Twenty-four houses had been arranged around the village green. The earliest were long houses made of timber built on stone, with roofs supported on crucks, followed after a stagnant interval by four terraces of long houses by the early fifteenth century, this time made of whinstone (for which the quarry was established) and clay to the full height of the walls. By 1675 the long houses were converted into small houses and byres. The excavation also revealed that people of the Iron Age had been living close by in round houses. Again, there is a spectacular array of rig and furrow ploughing around the settlement, which shows up brilliantly from the air.

A village that has disappeared because the owner decreed it is Bywell, when in the mid-nineteenth century the villagers were relocated at Stocksfield. This was of advantage to the creation of a lovely open space between some very fine and ancient churches, castle and hall, rather like the relocation of Ford village by Marchioness Waterford, but one wonders what the ordinary people who lived there thought about it all. Were they anxious to leave their homes? Did they have any say in the matter?

124 West Whelpington. *NUM*

125 Edlingham.

126 Near Bavington.

127 Dunstanburgh Castle. *Marion Clark*

Another example is Low Buston, near Warkworth. There is a lovely painted map made by Thomas Norton that shows how it lay in the seventeenth century. The hollow of the main street is still visible, with garden plots. It had eleven taxpayers, and by 1538 there was a defensive muster of thirty-one men, but it became a park around 1800.

This process of abandonment and closure also affected the village of Alnhamsheles, near Ingram in the Cheviot Hills. It is still possible to see the remains of the settlement there, when the earthworks are thrown into relief by deep shadows. There are about twenty rectangular buildings, some in enclosures and some with enclosures attached. It appears in documents in 1265, had eleven tenants in 1314, and was extended in the sixteenth century. The field systems, not only of that settlement, but of much earlier lynchets and terraces are all around the hillslopes and valleys, showing vividly how far agriculture changed there from grain-growing to animal pasture, leaving a fossilized record for us to read (Beckensall, 2003)

In contrast to villages based on agriculture, Carr Shield (or Carrshield) is the remnant of a mining village. Extending along a road, nestling in a valley protected to some extent from the worst of the weather, it has a Methodist chapel of 1857 at the north end, of a common design in this area, a school building of 1851 (significantly with separate boys' and girls' entrances) which became a field centre for schools, then – as most of these have now closed, the latest being at

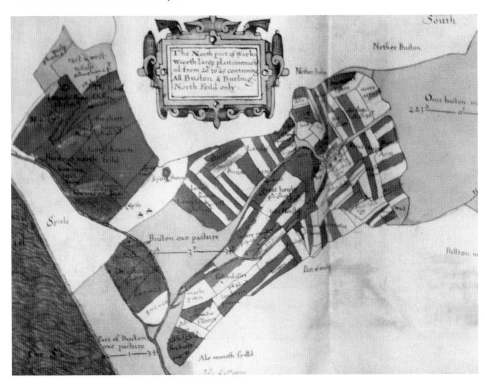

128 Thomas Norton's map of Low Buston.

129 Alnhamsheles, west of Ingram, looking over the site of the village to Ros Castle.

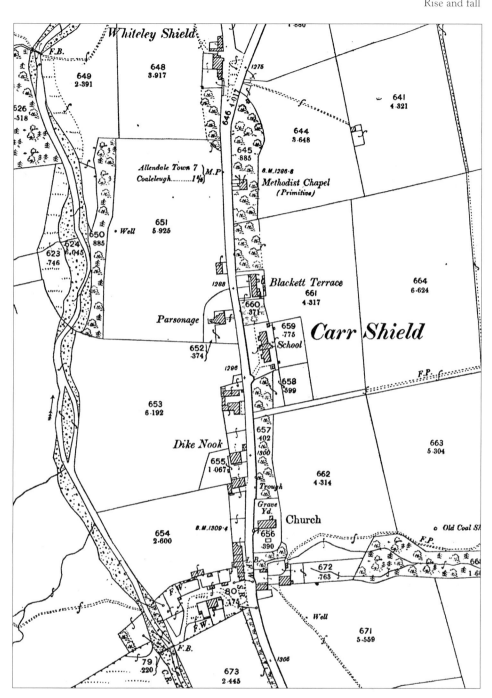

130 Map of the Carrshield area, 1860.

Catton – a private concern. A church built in 1822 was demolished, but the graveyard with unusual modern stones is accessible by steps leading up from the road. The mine manager's house has been refurbished, with an attractive garden developed – again, a happy effect of new people coming into the area. The village has a deeper past, though, as the mid-eighteenth century Whitely Shield Farm to the north has a ruined bastle house. So has Hartleycleugh, a mile further north. Many more of these defensive survivals have been recorded by Peter Ryder, from times when it was essential to protect life and property from roaming thieves.

The main reason for Carrshield's existence was lead, and the remains of this industry are still apparent to the south of the village, where mine offices, quarries, a miners' shop, blacksmith's shop and extensive workings are visible. There is also a small limekiln tucked away. Further south is the once-important lead-mining centre of Coalcleugh.

Without people, these communities would be just buildings and ruins to us. There are many ways in which we reach those who lived and worked there. One example will suffice. Bulmer's Directory of 1886, at a time when lead mining and smelting were folding up, describes Coalcleugh as 'a thriving village in mining days, but now contains only four families'. Under CarrShields it says that the 1822 church was erected by Mrs Diana Beaumont, the lady of the manor.

131 Carrshield school.

132 Carrshield chapel.

133 Abandoned workings and buildings between Carrshield and Coalcleugh.

> A chapel was erected here in 1704, by subscription among the miners; but on the completion of the present one the old chapel was converted into a school.

One therefore was provided from the miners' wages, the other from the rich owner. In the village the people who lived there included a gamekeeper, and Jonathan Shield kept a temperance hotel. There was a schoolmaster, a boot and clog maker, grocer and draper, butcher (and farmer) and a Mr Noble Sparke.

A few years later, in 1893, the school logbook gives us an insight into one event there. The local schoolmaster was worried about the dress and standards of his male pupil teacher. For three days in November he recorded that the pupil teacher's boots were dirty, and that he occasionally came without a collar, apparently 'by his father's orders'. On 17 November he records:

> Standard 1 children were examined. 5 were present. 3 did fairly well. 2 badly. Ment: Arith very fair, Gram. good (only nouns), Geog good. Shall have them in the hands of the Pupil Teacher and give him another trial. The work of the school is very satisfactory and it is a pleasure to have the hearty cooperation of the children, but very unsatisfactory to see a P. Teacher with dirty boots when the majority of the children are acting in harmony with the master's wishes. The average attendance (satisfactory) was 27.2.

On 20 November he records:

> The Pupil teacher has clean boots this morning. Attendance very bad. Nearly all the infants Std. 1 & 11 are absent owing to snow upon ground.

On 24 November:

> Examines Std. 1(?) on Thursday with splendid results.
> On Monday evening I reproved the P. Teacher for inflicting corporal punishment to his children. The punishment was given when my back was turned and I took the first opportunity that presented itself of trying to stop it. On Wednesday he deliberately struck Wll. Whitfield a violent blow on the cheek which was quite visible two hours afterwards. For this I reproved him at once, and shall lay the matter before the Managers of the School. For a long time corporal punishment by me has been unknown. Previous to this I have refused to inflict corporal punishment at the Pupil Teacher's request for trifles which ought not to exist if the teacher took pains to interest his children.

Readers will draw their own conclusions about the workings of the school and the character of those who were teaching.

There are some villages that, far from shrinking and disappearing, have adapted to change and expanded. Being in the commuter belt with access to places of employment by car has meant that they provide a domestic haven for those who do not wish to live in large towns or on estates. A place in the country can be bought by those who earn enough or are well-provided for in retirement. In some cases they may not mix in well with the existing community. Out of many examples, Felton will suffice.

Felton lies at an important river crossing, its early fifteenth-century bridge surviving in good condition, linking it with Thirston across the river – a settlement owned by the Duke of Northumberland's family.

Felton means a settlement established on cleared fields. It has buildings that point to an ancient foundation and continuous past, such as the complex church of St Michael on the hill to the west of the village. Its watermill, now preserved as a private house, may date to the thirteenth century, now with a Victorian house, cottages and stable block attached to it, converted in the 1980s. When I lived at Felton the waterwheel still worked, as there was expertise among the villagers to make it so. Weir, fish-pass and head-race channels led to the mill where three wheels used to turn.

Leading to it from the main street is a terrace of elegant two-storey houses of 1800, preceded by a seventeenth-century long house that is disguised by heavy 1960s restoration. Around the corner west towards the church and Felton Park is Gasworks Farm, built in the mid-nineteenth century to pipe gas up to the

134 Aerial view of Felton from the east.

main street where there was a brewery and public houses, for the street carried traffic on the Great North Road, wide enough then, flanked by a variety of stone houses, a bank, a reading room and chapel. A brick council estate and cemetery were added to the north of the old village at the end of fields, which still carry the S-bends of old rig and furrow systems of ploughing.

The hill from Thirston, over the old bridge and up the main street, was full of traffic until recently, the noise of grinding gears and the smoke of exhausts ever-present. A new bridge protected the old, which was closed. Such problems demanded a bypass. Before this was built, I remember a lorry-load of fish overturning (the driver was unhurt), and local people were encouraged to bring buckets to collect the catch. It made a change from rod and line.

The bypass put the village on a more vigorous commuter footing. Sites of a transport depot, a blacksmith's and the 'café sandpit' were taken over for new executive-type housing, and all the old property became desirable. The village school was already on a new site, and the increase in population ensured its survival, unlike others in the county. When the Millennium Fair was held, most of the village assembled for a photograph, taken from a mechanical hoist. There are many people of all ages, a sign that perhaps the future of this village community is assured.

135 A field full of fair folk: Felton villagers at the Millennium Fair.

136 Felton Fair, 2004: children watch Punch and Judy.

Most of the old Felton Hall has gone. Built in 1732, remodelled in 1799, and then partly demolished in 1951, what remains (the east wing) is still impressive. This overlooks the 'Riding Field', running down to the river, where there are still signs of its use in the Second World War. There is a fine eighteenth-century brick garden wall, a later greenhouse in splendid condition and a RC church of 1857 founded by Thomas Riddell. At the foot of a cross with a virgin and child, he holds a model of the church.

Felton remains an intriguing place, with its vast time range visible in hints and substance. The churchyard on the hill, crowded and extensive, has been well researched and published. There is still an active local history society, to which I belonged when I lived there. The vicarage, once a place where we rehearsed special services, has been sold and the Glebe Field has filled with new houses. The history of vicarages shows how rural communities, once served by vicars of some substance, status, and often private means, have been reorganised into pastoral groups with one priest to serve them.

Felton has retained its post office, but lost its bank, reading room and butcher's shop. It retains two of its inns, once so important to travellers along this busy highway. A redundant nonconformist church is now a private house, but the village hall has been renovated and the recreation ground retained. The village

137 Felton Park, 1820.

138 The change: as it is now.

boasts one of the finest annual fairs in the county because there are people with the will, belief and energy to retain and expand it. They even managed to get the Red Arrows to fly past, and the Boulmer helicopter and local microlights are frequent visitors to the fair. There are many stalls, food and drink in abundance, and first-class entertainment. It is a healthy sign that the village is truly alive, thanks to the efforts of a determined committee.

seven

The past in the present: pageants, plays and poetry

One powerful way of exploring the past is through improvised drama. The ready-made play may be the usual and quick way to re-enact scenes from history, but exploring themes with a group enables people to put themselves into someone else's shoes. The result may not be authentic 'history', but the past can become a little clearer and more relevant. As in all works of historical fiction, interpretation and the creation of the 'feel' of a period, based on selected facts, are worthy objectives. Possibilities are explored.

Many teachers have been involved in the improvisation process at many different levels. At a time when teachers gave up weekends to attend courses at Ford Castle to explore drama, so that they could carry what they had experienced back to the classroom, there were some memorable moments when for all of us a strong sense of reality crept into the process. This kind of course has become impossible for teachers today because of the vast amount of administrative work that has been forced upon them. Much of Ford Castle as it appears now is the result of restoration and development by the Marchioness Waterford. An accomplished artist, a rich widow from a powerful local family, a teetotaller (she closed the village pub) and philanthropist, she made the decision to move the old village out of sight of the castle and build a new one to the east on higher ground. Little is known about this event, but it was chosen by a group of teachers for dramatic improvisation. Her character, background and determination were considered from a number of sources, and one otherwise quiet woman in the group emerged in the role suggested; she became a Maggie Thatcher-type of handbagging authoritative figure used to having, and determined to have, her own way on that issue. The local vicar, Hastings Neville, who has left books including *A Corner of the North* (1909) and a forelock-tugging account of his patron, we imagined became caught between his dependency on her and his concern for the local people. They might not have wished to be moved from

139 Ford Castle.

homes that they had grown up in, even though something supposedly better was on offer. The teacher who took on this role was many years later to become an Anglican priest in this county! We pictured the defiance of some villagers, but they were really up against it. One local, it is recorded, was noticeably absent from church on many occasions, so she offered to buy him a horse to make sure he had no excuse for not attending. We didn't find the outcome in any document. So we all began to slip into our roles, with grumbling, defiance, awe and fear in the air. One became the estate manager, another a visitor, and the canvas became colourful.

All this insight into a scarcely documented event that to the local people would have been more important than most other things that were happening in the second part of the nineteenth century made everyone aware of the importance of the untold parts of history. During the same weekend another group was learning to use the new video recorder that had just started to make an impact. The site of the Battle of Flodden lies close to Ford – so close that James IV of Scotland spent his last night of life at the castle. The Border has a history quite unlike that of the rest of the country, with its own set of rules to cope with turbulence and the tug of war between England and Scotland. It also has its own poetry, the Border Ballads, a distinctive literary genre. On this occasion in 1513 it was full-scale battle, not a local skirmish, and the slaughter in hand-to-hand fighting and the massacre of those defeated was appalling. The little church at Branxton, still there today, became a temporary mortuary for over a thousand dead. Thousands of mutilated corpses were strewn over a mile of battlefield.

A local folk singer, Terry Conway, who worked for the roadworks department of the county council, gave an evening talk on Border Ballads, which he also sang – a stunning performance that inspired the 'crew' to take the camera with him to Flodden. At the end of the course, when all the different groups performed their work, we were left to watch the scene as the camera caught the drops of rain trickling from the blood-red berries in the hedgerows near the Flodden cross. *The Flowers of the Forest* was sung as a background. I remember that there was hardly a dry eye, with the thought of all the wasted lives, the folly and inhumanity of the rich and powerful, some of it centred on this castle where we worked and thought about the past. The body of King James was not found until the day after the battle. It was found stripped and covered with wounds, recognised, and taken to Berwick. The body lay for years unburied at Sheen, Richmond, and after the dissolution of the monasteries was found in a lumber room among the rubbish, where 'workmen there for their foolish pleasure, hewed off his head'. Where it eventually ended up is unknown. The fate of the remains of the soldiers of the armies was no less gruesome. Those who like to think of battles as being glorious should read the details of Flodden. Those who take sides from a distance would do well to remember that the memorial on Piper's Hill is inscribed to the dead of both nations. If we try to find out what happened in the past, we must approach the shadows with open minds.

140 Branxton: Flodden.

Some of my most enjoyable moments working with children have been exploring many themes, either in lesson time or as out-of-school activity. Not many schools pursue this to such an extent, as worksheets, imposed curricula and preparations for tests have driven out much creativity. It has even become necessary to formalise 'thinking skills'. Young people who are working on improvisation are thinking because they are faced with choices, decisions. These skills can be explored in many ways, of which drama is one. Sometimes it works like this: after an initial 'warm up', groups of children would get to work on their chosen themes and stories, or on stories told to them. One example that I have found particularly valuable is Brecht's *The Caucasian Chalk Circle*. It is based on one of the judgements of Solomon: two women claimed the same living baby. Both gave birth at the same time, but one baby had died. Solomon ordered the child to be cut in half so that each mother could have her share. One woman refused and gave up her rights to the child. Solomon judged her love to be stronger; she deserved the child.

Brecht refashioned this story, set it in a time of civil war, when a baby heir to the principality was abandoned by his rich mother and the whole court. A young servant girl, overcome by love at the expense of her own safety, fled with the child to the mountains, pursued by soldiers who had orders to kill it. She married a man whom she thought was dying, so that she could give a respectable name to the child, only to find that she had an active husband. Thus she had to live, kept going by caring for the child until peace had been restored. The 'true' mother returned, the child was traced and abducted. A trial followed in which the unorthodox judge of the day heard the cases of the two women. He ordered the child to be brought in and placed inside a circle drawn in chalk on the floor, and ordered the women to test the strength of their love by pulling the child out of the circle by his arm. The aristocratic woman won the tug of war, so the judge gave the child to the other who really loved and cared for him.

This is the very stuff of drama with purpose. Too often children are expected to jump through hoops, take part in productions (especially musicals) where everything is cut and dried for them by adults and in which they have little to do with anything except their parts. At worst it is about dressing up and showing off, with the most talented getting the best parts. But what happens when you begin to discuss questions like these:

When is the story set? Could it be now?

What would make a mother abandon her child? What about all the other people around her? Would they think the child worth risking their lives for?

Why did the servant girl choose peril for the sake of a child who was not her own? What was going on in the minds of the soldiers who were pursuing her with orders to kill a baby?

Why should a man pretend to be dying in order to marry a young girl?

What arguments would the two women use in court to put forward their cases of ownership?

What kind of person was the judge?

141 and *142* Involvement in drama: young people from Corbridge Middle School rehearsing *The Chalk Circle* in 1978. *Karen Melvin*

This, of course, is not all that can be teased out of the situation, but it is a start. The young people are going to find other matters of concern in this story. Single parents and unmarried mothers are common enough, for example. Any teacher will see here an opportunity to explore not just a story from or about the past, but to explore values – and this is a process in which everyone can take part.

From the initial improvisations that included an episode where 'Maria' and her baby arrive at an inn to find there is no room there, they are faced with the fine rich women who despise her. They are not used to inconvenience and squalor, for their lives are lived in a protected world. Or take the soldiers who were pursuing Maria. In an improvisation, the question of whether or not to obey orders blindly because 'they' tell us to do so are challenged by the soldier who has children of his own and would not kill a baby.

The toadies and sycophants who surround the prince (the child's father) and his lady at the baptism of the baby when the civil war suddenly broke loose at the palace gates was an exploration delightful to observe. The character of the judge, his humanity, unorthodoxy and wisdom, was expressed in little playlets that the youngsters devised, with cases for him to solve. It is when improvisation reaches a point where it is worth fashioning into a well-made play that it needs professional help, as young people are seldom ready or prepared to do this. This is where language may be written to take them beyond the normal, to extend their vocabulary and ideas. It is also an opportunity to involve more people in the creative process by involving them in staging, sound and other technical devices that make the play more vivid to its audience. At Belford Middle School, for example, the young people were encouraged to choose images from works of art as a back-projection to the story. Breughel, for example, for the wedding feast. Maria was filmed on the nearby moor running away with the child in her arms from the soldiers. This was projected on to a screen for the performance. Music was carefully chosen to fit the mood. At Hexham for the Abbey Festival, one school undertook a dance-drama introduction to each scene, playing out the theme to come. Many schools were involved in the production, including a ceilidh band and choir from Rothbury; they sang from the back of the packed Queen's Hall and played on stage for Irish-type dancers for the 'wedding' of Maria. How can we evaluate the effect of this shared experience of drama on those young people, being an integral part of such an important theme? The act of watching what others had decided and careful listening to the dialogue was a great experience.

If a play is to be set in the past there is a whole world to be explored of what people wore, where they lived, how much they earned and what their money would buy, what they ate, what they did for entertainment and so much more. The play did not become a re-enactment of the past, but the past was there to show that no matter what differences there were in lifestyles, human thought, passion and values have remained important. 'What do we value most in life?' is a question devoutly to be asked.

143 Rothbury children with their Spindlestone Dragon at Cragside (for the *Radio Times*). The play, based on improvisation, was performed by the children on Radio Newcastle.

To take a more recent example at Hexham Middle School, a well-known local story lends itself to similar treatment. A party of raiders with the Robson surname made a foray into Liddesdale, stole sheep, and drove them to north Tynedale. When they got them home they realised that they were 'scabbed' and spread the disease to the Robson sheep. They returned to the place where they had stolen them, blamed the people there for allowing them to be in this condition, took seven of the most important Grahams prisoner, and hanged them! The Robsons warned that 'the neist tyme gentlemen cam to tak their schepe, they war not to be scabbit!' After a visit to the local Border Museum, which helped to provide a background to time and place, the pupils were encouraged to go beyond the factual to look at moral issues. Examples of the kinds of questions asked were partly factual (such as where are Liddesdale and Tynedale; what are ewes, mutton and scab?). Then the questions were on the lines of what a family diet was in the sixteenth century, what constituted a family group, how was meat kept in the winter and – quite a different question – what kind of law and order authorities did they have?

From this the pupils raised questions about whether family loyalty was important, how far they would be prepared to break the law for their family, whether it was right to steal food if you were starving, whether it was right to blame people for your problems and was it right to take revenge? As the reiver group that had done the stealing was so incensed to find that the sheep were scabby, does it make things worse to be made a fool of in front of other people?

PAGEANT

In contrast to this use of the past in drama is the pageant; it has played a role in the life of many towns and villages. On the whole I am not inclined to become involved in pageants, where people dressed in cardboard cut-out costumes as Roman soldiers parade, wear swords and utter some words of Latin. It is much better to watch the Ermine Street Guard handle this kind of thing. The pageant as a genre generally is a static affair, with tableaux representing various events in history. Change the period; change the tableau; Viking, Victorian. Not so the pageants at Warkworth, and again I draw on personal experience.

In the late 1970s I was drawn into a revival of the Warkworth Pageant. At a time when Alnwick College of Education, where I worked, was doomed to be the first to close, a project on this scale centred on one of the finest castles and villages in England was a godsend. The local people were determined to revive a tradition that died out before the Second World War. It is schemes of this sort that keep villages alive and pulsating. Nearby Felton village today pulls everyone together in the community with an annual fair that attracts hundreds of visitors. Warkworth chose drama. It was full of talented people – historians, stonemasons,

144 Warkworth Castle and bridge, 1820s.

farmers, artists, musicians, for example. There were many young people eager to take part and there was a strong corporate spirit.

The Warkworth Drama Group was formed in 1974 with the aim of furthering community spirit in Warkworth and its district 'through drama productions, readings and village pageants'. It began with dramatic productions, moved on to Son et Lumiere in the church and then on to a pageant.

Archives revealed a succession of pageants where photographs suggested a highly formalised series of episodes in history, costumed and grouped accordingly. Newspapers of the time showed what appeared to be largely tableaux, with some narration. A paid pageant master had been appointed for this, and groups such as the W.I. were invited to perform country dances.

That was the past, but what should be done for the future? The producer (Joan Hellawell) called a group of us together – a nucleus for ideas and planning. A period of about 100 years was chosen, beginning with the castle being handed over to the Percys by Edward III, focussing on such figures as Harry Hotspur and events such as the Battle of Otterburn and culminating in the defeat at Shrewsbury of the Percys and submission to Henry IV. A framework of events was laid down, but it was discussion on what could be included within that outline that made the event successful. All ages, all talents, varied experience and above all considerable enthusiasm would be focused on this project.

145 Warkworth Castle.

146 At the start of a recent pageant.

Warkworth Castle is a Percy stronghold, along with Alnwick and Prudhoe. Shakespeare has made one of the family stand out, in his depiction of Harry Hotspur through his hot-headed valour, whose life contrasted with that of Prince Hal and his dissolute companions. Hotspur's farewell to his wife before he leaves for the decisive, and fatal for him, Battle of Shrewsbury, is a fine moment in drama, chosen to be part of the events. Also from Shakespeare came the prediction made by Richard II of civil war and chaos that would follow the death of an anointed king, to be spoken with power and passion from the steps leading down from the castle.

But history is about more than those who have had a large part in shaping its destiny. What about the ordinary, anonymous folk whose toil and lives made it possible for those above them to carry out their ambitions? Very well, there are some who have no memorial, but who did the building and the fighting? What did the building of such a large castle mean to them? What did they know outside their own narrow boundaries? (Colour 21)

An idea began to take shape to unify time and themes. It had already been decided to include that superb tale of Chaucer's Pardoner, about the three Rioters who went in search of death and found it through avarice. These three became the focal point we were looking for. Two farmers and the head of a local middle school had superb local Northumberland voices (quite different from

147 Richard II.

'Geordie') and great zest. They would entertain the Percys and their guests with the Pardoner's Tale, they would fight at Otterburn and return defeated, and when labour was needed for building the castle, guess who would provide it? They would witness the downfall of Harry Hotspur and subjugation to Henry IV. They would be in from the beginning and, when events had run their course, they would still be there. They were everyone; they were past, present and future.

At one stage the present intruded in a marked way. A local builder, who was in the audience, had demolished the Magdalene chapel site, now built over, and a Pedlar who was telling the children the story of the Spindlestone Dragon while all were awaiting news of Otterburn, worked this into his narrative with promises of supernatural doom for such an act of desecration! The Rioters took every opportunity to chaff the crowd, pointing out people they knew in the audience. There was music, dance, mime and even a horse made its appearance.

There was armour and banners, and the battle that eventually forced Warkworth Castle into submission was a fantastic pyrotechnic display by the local RAF. Many of these successful elements have remained in subsequent pageants, now held every three years. (Colour 24, 25)

The whole pageant grew as it went along. A memorable moment came from a stonemason who had discussed with the producer what he would tell the audience about castle-building, what it was for and how it was built. He took centre stage as the children behind mimed or played at being builders; his rich Northumberland speech was potent and relevant: he really knew what he was talking about.

Costumes and props began to appear. The most important thing of all was not how well people looked the part, but whether they could be heard. In the open air this problem of audibility is a nightmare, solved in this case by the actors speaking up with powerful voices, and by their moving always as close as possible to the audience.

To stage such an ambitious work was one thing; to attract large audiences for the whole week was crucial. A good start was that with the whole village involved there was a ready-made audience. The actors themselves were audience throughout – part of the concept of production. It was decided to hold it for six nights, so news had to be broadcast. This literally happened, as radio and television took it up with gusto, as of course did the press. A slick publicity machine was set up. During the Alnwick Fair – another traditional and highly successful local event – some of the cast invaded the marketplace there, and one of the Rioters was sentenced to the ducking stool. Meanwhile, costumed characters, some with musical instruments, joined the throng of visitors. This happily drew attention to both events, and tourists used miles of film. Posters of impeccable taste were produced and displayed.

There are many memories for those who were involved over twenty-six years ago (surely it's not that long?). For example, at an evening dress rehearsal soldiers were trying out their costumes as the light faded. Some were walking along the

148 Ready for battle.

149 1977s finale.

150 A Warkworth 'Rioter' in the ducking stool at Alnwick Fair, 1977.

battlements when a scream came from below. An American lady was convinced that she had seen ghosts and was quite shattered by the experience. Among the cast, the children were quite extraordinary: properly motivated and supervised and present throughout the action on each night, they enjoyed every moment of it, anticipating the lines and events in their body language. The whole village and its surrounding area came together in a way that is rare, and the traders loved it.

This is one way of bringing the past to life. There was early discussion about life and times. At the time of Harry Hotspur, what did people eat? Where did the people live? What was their life expectancy? To have Professor Tony Tuck living in the village and working in the group was the use of one expert among many. The script that emerged was a truly combined effort, and the process of introducing this large potential cast was skilfully handled by the producer and others.

The pageant ran from 1–6 August in 1977. To give some idea of how times have changed, a beautifully printed programme cost 15p. Tickets were 60p for adults and 30p for others. Performances began at 8.30 p.m. because the special lighting effects and the final battle relied on darkness. Wild geese flew overhead. The south front of the castle was a thing to be wondered at, and attention was constantly drawn to different parts of the performance area. The cast was announced as The Villagers of Warkworth. The action was listed as:

Episode 1: (1328-1332) The scene moves from Warkworth Castle to Westminster, where King Edward III grants Henry Percy the castle and lordship of Warkworth. The villagers celebrate his return.
Episode 2: (1377) Henry Percy's grandson, whom Richard II created the first Earl of Northumberland, built the keep that you see today.
Episode 3: (1388)
The Battle of Otterburn.
Episode 4: (1399)
After the Percys help to depose Richard II, he prophesies that they will in turn rebel against Henry Bolinbroke (Henry IV).
The villagers help to entertain important guests at the castle with a play.
Episode 5: (1403-1405)
King Richard's prophecy is fulfilled. Harry Hotspur leads the rebels against King Henry and is defeated at the Battle of Shrewsbury.
King Henry besieges Warkworth Castle; it surrenders and Henry takes away the earl's lands and title.

Shadows of the past certainly took on substance. The programme, which was my responsibility to devise, brought together our aims, printed in these words:

Warkworth, named after a woman, Werce, owes its beginnings as a village to its strong defensive position. The river Coquet makes a big loop before flowing out to sea, and on the promontory formed in this loop the village slopes down from the south where the castle stands. The pattern of castle, main street with its long thin gardens at right angles, church, marketplace and bridge has changed very little. Modern developments lie generally outside this ancient nucleus.

You visitors to the castle will be aware of its strong position at once. What you may also notice is that the original 'motte and bailey' design covered a slightly larger area on the eastern sea-facing side; the present eastern wall has been drawn in.

The history of the village is obviously tied up with the history of the castle and its owners. In one sense the 'ordinary' people did not have much control over what happened to them; they were called on to serve their lord, they had all kinds of obligations in peace and war.

In another sense, though, they had their own private lives – their loves, hates, service to others, petty quarrels with neighbours – and all the other things that still make up the life of any community. Of course, their lives were different from ours in so many ways, but we are still like them.

This unchanging fact of human life is the basis of the pageant. We have taken what we know of one part of Warkworth's history, selected the outstanding events, compressed time and place, and are re-presenting this to you. Many things we cannot do: we cannot re-create the speech of the time, for example, but we can try to recapture its flavour in our own local dialect. We cannot convince you that today is yesterday, but we can use devices of costume and music to create a partial illusion. We all know that we are watching a play, so we don't mind coming forward to the audience to remind you of this.

The historical facts are set out below. These are one basis for the pageant. The second basis is Chaucer's 'The Pardoner's Tale', chosen because it was written close enough to the time of our action and because its theme is timeless: that people destroy themselves through their own greed, no matter what their status in life. We have adopted the three Rioters who go out in search of death and have turned themselves into more than something out of Chaucer's story. They are everyone: people who get caught up in political and economic events not of their own choosing, who fight the battles of Otterburn or Shrewsbury; who die at Ypres, Stalingrad or in Northern Ireland. Uncle Sam, Kitchener or the Earl of Northumberland call them away and they perform acts of incredible bravery, self-sacrifice, bestiality, love and hate in the terrible contradiction that we all are. The call to arms may be unavoidable, but how man behaves once he has been called cannot be blamed on others. Shakespeare's Henry V, when he wanders disguised among his men on the night before Agincourt, cannot shoulder responsibility for everything; must all the legs and arms chopped off in battle be his fault? He argues that his soldiers' souls are their own, that they are accountable for themselves.

So the past is never glorious: it is too cruel, too bloody. It is easy to forget that in this Border country, when all is so peaceful, violence and sudden death could descend at any minute. The scatter of castles and towers, the lack of elegant buildings, the solid functional quality of everything speak of a hard life, yet this is only part of the story. There was happiness, laughter, music, dancing, and celebrations. We hope we have balanced the conflicting elements in our pageant.

The pageant was one way in which history came to life. On a different scale was an event planned by the Northumberland National Park Authority and the County Council, called *A Living History of Northumberland*, as part of the Millennium celebrations. Ten Northumberland middle schools each studied a different key period in the county's history. An exhibition in the Millennium Dome was one outcome, and the finale was a 'Living History' pageant at Alnwick Castle and town in June 2000.

A group of actors, closely working with staff, went to schools and performed scenes from the periods chosen or allocated to the various schools to give the flavour of the periods. These ranged from the Celtic Iron Age to *A Sustainable Future: 2100 AD*, with ten episodes in all. Each school produced something different, but had in common a detailed investigation into some aspect of life, such as domestic routine and crafts. The colourful and poignant work was exhibited as the pupils and staff supported their displays with their live presence, continuing their investigation in role. At Alnwick there was a long procession of all the groups through the town, part of a much larger procession of great colour and variety. Then the action moved to the castle grounds, where we were entertained with playlets as well as the exhibition, including 'The Scabby Sheep' already referred to.

The results of all this were saved to some extent on a video.

151 Part of the middle schools' procession leaves Alnwick Castle.

152 Students and staff of St Cloud University dress for the occasion.

Investigating the past through drama makes it vivid for many, and especially for those who are lucky enough to take part in it. It may not be authentic history, as so much must be imagined, but then 'authentic history' too is a questionable concept, with many different interpretations of what happened in the past. Many schools and groups continue to work hard to make it a living thing for others.

A recent 're-enactment' of the Hexham Riot of 1761 (Beckensall 2001, Corfe 2004) in the marketplace involved local adults and children in workshops, which included singing, to bring to mind one of the most disturbing and bloody documented events in the history of this town.

Over 5,000 people had gathered in and around Hexham in 1761 from many parts of the country, to protest against the ballot for the militia. After the reading of the Riot Act, the Yorkshire Militia opened fire on the crowds and about fifty people were killed. The re-enactment had an important part to play in keeping this part of history alive, especially an event that seems to have been ignored. It had the advantage of raising all kinds of issues, such as the right of people to protest when faced with an apparently unfair conscription into the army – even though an army might be deemed necessary to the security of the Realm.

153 Hexham Riot re-enactment, 2004. *Colin Dallison*

POETRY

We may wonder whether we exist or not. Descartes' answer was 'I think and therefore I am'. That leads me to wonder how I experience the past; the past can only exist in my consciousness. I bring it to life by knowing about it, by thinking about it. Possibly when I am dead that past no longer exists. The world can only exist because we experience it. 'I am, therefore everything around me exists'.

Things continue to exist only through living people; the dead and the past exist through us. A piece of music conceived centuries ago is relived by being played in the present. To thousands who have never heard it, it cannot exist.

When I was commissioned to write some poems to accompany a performance of Buxtehude's *Membra Jesu Nostri* I had not heard the music. People had kept it alive, and were continuing to do so by arranging to perform it again. Today the actual performance can be kept alive on a disc as well as in notation on paper or other material. My words at the time of performance can be kept alive through a recording, yet in the past this was impossible. Most of what we say in our lives disappears into thin air.

I read these poems in Hexham Abbey at a candlelit performance in 2003. They were not a translation of the Latin words that Buxtehude used, but a personal reflection on the material that inspired the music; parts of the body of Christ as he hung on the cross.

I have often thought about those ballad writers of old, particularly those who celebrated for the tribe feats of heroism, in which they linked the stories to the antecedents of those who took part. Long epics were memorised and repeated on occasions, handed down to whoever would listen. It might be the *Odyssey*, *Beowulf* or a Border Ballad. The narrator and singer were revered, and admired for their phenomenal memories. Some people today continue to memorise their long, complex genealogies because these are important to their identities now. Their histories survive because they care so much.

If I lost my poems and there were no other copies, I should not be able to rewrite then exactly as they were. Where my poems come from, I'm not sure. Sometimes they seem to write themselves, although they must be part of a little-understood process of ideas being mulled over, sometimes subconsciously.

Imagine the setting where the poems came to life: Hexham Abbey with candles giving off their flickering light, shadows, a warm glow not altogether constant. An orchestra of baroque-type instruments, a choir and young soloists, all of high quality. It was there in a full performance that the impact of the music came to me.

154 Hexham pulpit.

I began with this:

Body

Christ's body hammered to a cross,
Head bowed in agony, scalp shredded
By compressed, twisted thorns;
Arms stretched out wide, encompassing a world
Of suffering, world of wrong.
Fierce struggle of heart's blood to circulate.

Constricted limbs give up the ghost.
His body, caught between our earth and heaven
Awaits submission from his final, fading words
When 'It is finished' drops from stiffened lips.
The plea of 'Let this cup of sorrow pass from me'
Had dissipated in the darkening air.
God would not let this be, for
Every body part was doomed
To suffer all the pain the world had ever known,
Focussing then and now and future in one place,
Before the sealing of a tomb, before release to heaven.

Veil of the temple torn, his body torn,
Darkness covering the earth,
Darkness at the centre of our hearts –
Mankind's consent to evil done in our name.

The rest was interspersed at appropriate times, following music and ancient words. The audience did not have a copy until after the performance; they had to listen, and the poems had to have an immediacy. Two of them now follow.

Knees

The Romans were accomplished torturers,
For Empire rests on fear.
A little ledge was added to the wooden cross
So that the body weight would not allow the nails to tear right through the hands,
Giving Christ more time to suffer and to die.
His knees were bent at their imperial command.
So far the torturers had it all their way –
But matters did not end in pain and death.

Knees fold to take our weight in prayer,
In supplication and surrender to a higher force
Than earthly principalities and powers.
We know, for all our arrogance, our earthly aspiration,
That we are but dust.
The Dance of Death dooms emperors and prelates, chimneysweepers equally.
And so we kneel, attempting a surrender
That will open up reluctant minds and spirits,
Link finite with the infinite,
Make Christ's cross and open tomb
A symbol of the hope that we have grasped
When it was set before us.

His knees were bent in rigor mortis when his body separated from the cross.
It is less effort for those of us he left behind
To kneel before that cross,
But, oh, so difficult to reach our God in prayer,
To make complete surrender to His will.

155 St Peter.

Face

We have no say in our choice of face: accept what you are born with.
You may
Rage against beauty always denied, nose too long, lips too thin,
Or find (oh ecstasy!) you have a face that fits the current cover magazine.
Those with the cash can have a face lift, pumped up lips that glisten silicone
Yet, like adolescents, never see reflections of themselves as satisfactory.
In many ways we 'prepare a face to meet the faces that we meet':
The practised smile, contemptuous aside, a jutting jaw,
Stiff upper lip, are postures that we think
Will place us in the driving seat.

The routemaps of our lives appear in lines
When gentle passage of serenity, moments of deep gravity,
Ascents through strife, bereavement, poverty, depravity
Cannot be liquidated by a bottled remedy.

Perhaps it is the mouth and eyes that say it all:
A tight-lipped bitterness or a flowing ease,
Half moon turned-down disapproval,
Upturned happiness dimpling cheeks with smiles.

It is the eyes that mirror most our souls.
Glazed false serenity of addict's dazed dilation
In choosing an escape that only makes things worse.
Eyes easily angered leap to life when raw nerves fire.
Eyes, soft and warm surge sympathy from wells of deep commitment and content.
Lovers lock lives and passion eye to eye.
Ashamed, our eyes slide sideways to an empty space.

We thus betray an inner life or open up a terrifying emptiness inside.
The body's fountainhead, the brain,
More complex than anything invented by itself
Controls our feelings and our thoughts.
No matter how the face prepares itself
Or is prepared cosmetically
Truth pushes through to show us and our neighbours what we are.

Artists have sought to paint and sculpt the face of Christ,
Leaving a legacy of images largely of his triumph or his suffering.
Some have drained the face of character, leaving it bland and vacuous.
There must be other pictures in our minds:

We see Christ striding through the Temple precinct
Where a rabble of commercial interests angered him,
Rich merchants squeezing through the camel's eye.
We see a face to match the overturning of the tables,
Rage at desecration of his Father's house,
Purging of a den of thieves.
We see his tears and sense his choking throat when Lazarus was dead,
When Jesus wept not just for the general sins of all the world
But for the focal point of one lost friend.
How often do we see amid a mission of deep seriousness
A growing smile upon his lips, rich laughter in his eyes?

We ask the lord to lift up the light of his countenance upon us,
Yet what must have happened when he turned full gaze upon
One singled out, commanding 'Follow me'?
A current must have surged like purgatorial fire
From eye to eye, when time stood still.
There was no choice but to obey.
And after that, the calm, the certainty,
That what was spoken from the depth of Jesus' eyes

156 Hexham Abbey: Antiphon.

Would never let us be the same,
Would never leave us comfortless,
Never let us go,
Be with us to the end of time.

During this performance one could take in the building itself, with its high gothic arches, fifteenth-century painting, modern extensions and renovations, bits and pieces of centuries from Roman to funerary hatchments. There have been some previous times for me when a surfeit of the some period music has sent my mind to dwell on how candle wax melts, what shapes are formed, what parts of surrounding stone are illuminated. We sit in a building that was founded in the 670s, one of the first great Anglo-Saxon buildings of England, the earliest part of which is now reduced to a crypt and to fragments of sculpture. Perhaps, for some, the shadows of the past are strongly present here.

In what seems another world and another time, when my very grown up son was only five, he said something that really impressed me. I had given him a torch that delighted him and he said, 'Into all the dark places I will look with this torch.' Words take root and from them ideas grow.

Dark and Secret Places

Into all the dark places
I will look with this torch.
The cupboard underneath the stairs
May be a charnel house
Or resting-place for ghosts
Where giant spiders lurk
With glowing eyes and sticky legs.
But I will scare them all away
So they will go next door,
And I shall never see them any more.
This little beam will laser out
The Daleks in the attic,
Burglars hiding underneath my bed,
Fresh scalps hanging in the chimney,
Pits with spikes and moving walls.
What is dead will stay dead.

Into all the dark places
I will look with this torch;
Beam it through cavities of trees
To where the owl sits brooding
With solemn and saucerous eyes;

Thrust it through molehills' volcanic tops,
Catch the scamper of soft shovel feet;
Embody the disembodied
Flutter of wings from shadowy bushes,
Light up the river,
The plop of the pebble dislodged.
Mist-covered moon will be mine
As I startle the night-flying clouds.
My beam will dance ahead of me and be my eyes.
But I will only see in part.
Hand, governed by my will,
Illuminates a tiny fraction at a time.
Returning darkness closes over what I've seen;
The phantoms have returned –
The bush again becomes a bear.

There is over thirty years between this poem and the others. Poetry can provide a kind of diary of experiences. If you live in a place for a while, something of its past must impress and tantalise. At the beginning of its history, Hexham was distinguished by its building, erected by Wilfrid, one of the great power-figures of his age. But before that, what? No one knows, but the name 'Hagustaldes ea ham' suggests a young Anglian of the warrior class, unable to inherit land because he was the younger son, settling by the river. But what was it like there when Queen Etheldreda gave Wilfrid land and income to build the priory? I had to imagine that part of the story:

Hexham: The Forerunners

Out of the river mist we saw our landing site,
As wild geese broke the silence with their hurried flight.
A curling thread of woodsmoke shimmered from a dark, coned roof,
Carrying a scent of fragrant cooking drifting towards fields
Won from woodland clearings and from burnt-out scrub.

We hauled our raft ashore and toiled along the track
That led from riverbank to settlement.
Rough farmers stumbled down the slope to meet with us,
Fingering their spades and hoes in challenge to our right.

'We speak for Etheldreda, Queen, and for your new lord Wilfrid.'

Such words had their effect, there was no one to dare
To voice a disagreement with the power of Church and State.

They knew the limitations of their role in life.
Theirs to plough, to till, to sow, to reap the harvest of their toil;
Theirs to secure the boundaries of fields,
To keep their beasts from harm in pastures close to home;
Theirs to protect their wives and bairns;
Theirs to obey, or break out in a rage
When what they built up, what they loved
Was doomed or under threat.

'We come in peace. We bring good news.'

Could any news from that far land of Church and State be good?

'You have a chance to walk with God, to build His temple in this place.'

We had already made a choice of land to build our church:
There on the hill, flanked by the streams that fed the Tyne.

'Hagustaldesham, now famous in the eyes of men
Is where you share the glory and the power.'

That's what we told them, yet we knew
What all the coming changes meant to them:
A higher price for food, a ready market close at hand,
Work in the quarries, work to fashion stone,
Work with timber, jobs for all at home.

They wanted to know more; we squatted in their dismal huts,
Stared at by finger-sucking bairns
And drank the proffered, bitter brew.
We told them of the plans, the wondrous transformation of their land,
Of Wilfrid's vision of the rising church
To meet God in the clouds of Hexham's skies.
We offered gifts, for we had come prepared
And knew before we left that soon from miles around
The hunters and the herdsmen, farmers, those with skill
Would make their way from hills and woods and fields
To do God's work, and benefit themselves.

The rest of our knowledge varies, sometimes detailed, sometimes with huge blanks, like so much of early history. When nothing dramatic happens, that is not news. The unusual and sensational are of more interest. All rich ecclesiastical establishments in insecure areas were vulnerable to raids, attracted by their riches.

157 A replica of the Lindisfarne Gospels on the Abbey Frith Stool (or Bishop's Throne).

Hexham was at the heart of the Border country, and from Viking times onwards there was a history of violence. From the thirteenth century onwards English and Scottish troops plundered and marched from time to time.

The shadows of the past were now caused by flames of destruction. Vikings had been operating long before this, when portents of dragons were seen in the sky. Yet something arose out of this uneasy area; for a while Northumbria was a centre of international learning and culture.

But Northumberland became a frontier zone, with its own laws and justice. That mafia called 'Reivers' stamped itself on the land. I dip into hundreds of years among all the unease and violence and find something to remind me that the sensational and violent are not the whole picture. The Anglo-Saxon Alcuin of York's writing has always impressed me. At the end of a group of short plays called *Shepherds, Rogues and Angels*, produced for the abbey in 1995, I gave to the 'Visitor' who had been sent to assess the spiritual health of the community in the fourteenth century words that had partly come from St Hilary (315-367) and from Alcuin (*Shepherds, Rogues and Angels*).

Alcuin was one of the giants of the eighth century. Like so many of the famous thinkers and doers of his day he came from a noble family, being trained in a monastic school at York that had been founded by one of Bede's pupils.

Alcuin took over the school, and made frequent visits to Rome – following the path of so many others, such as Wilfrid. There was nothing insular about these early scholars and innovators, for they were in touch with their European counterparts, sharing their knowledge and skills, a two-way process.

If we consider the impact of, for example, the Northumbrian School in its design and execution of manuscripts, so essential to the spread of Christianity in a pagan world, and if we marvel at the quality of the Lindisfarne Gospels, we understand something of the importance and flavour of the world inherited by Alcuin.

Alcuin met Charlemagne, who offered him the headship of the palace school at Achen. He became the emperor's adviser on doctrine, his agent in his dealings with the English, and eventually died in 804 at St Martin's at Tours, where he was abbot. Over 300 of his letters survive, biographies, poems and treatises on education, and his scriptorium at Tours reproduced texts in multiple copies in a world that clamoured for them. Throughout, he carried all that he had learned in Northumbria to enrich European scholarship. Lindisfarne, Jarrow and York may seem remote from Europe, but theyhave exercised a considerable influence there.

eight

A land of violence

Some writers give an anodyne view of history. Merrie England, knights in shining armour, the splendour of kings and queens, glorious victories abroad may be for some a way out of the ghastly reality of what people experienced. It is common for people to think themselves into the past as the aristocrat and not as the peasant, the victor and not the vanquished.

Northumberland has had as much of the horrors of history as anywhere else. Richard Fletcher's investigation in *Bloodfeud: Murder and Revenge in Anglo-Saxon England* (Fletcher 2002) begins with the murder of Earl Uhtred in 1016 with the collusion of King Canute (known to generations of school children for getting his feet wet at the seaside) – an event that led to sixty years of violence. It was a world of mafia thugs, of ambition, betrayal and sudden death that did not go away from the Borders for centuries. In 1006, for example, during the reign of King Ethelred (the 'ill-advised') a Scots army invaded Northumbria, burning and slaughtering, until it reached Durham. Waltheof, Earl of the Northumbrians, had shut himself away in Bamburgh Castle, perhaps feeling too old to do battle, but his son Uhtred rallied an army of Northumbrians and Yorkshire people and slaughtered the Scots. The chronicler, writing of this event sixty years after Uhtred's death, tells of what followed:

> Uhtred had the heads of the dead made more presentable with their hair braided, as was then the custom, and transported to Durham; there they were washed by four women, and fixed on stakes round the ramparts. They gave the women who had washed the heads a cow each in payment.

People are fascinated by horror, and some stories have been told over and over again in a time when peace seems to keep a need alive for the dominance of murder mysteries on our television screens, of films that explore cannibalism and science fantasy that reconstructs our worst nightmares.

There are some highlights – if that is the right term – well known in Northumberland, and one in particular is marked by the constant renewal of a wooden head that hangs from Winter's Gibbet close to the village of Elsdon. People tend to steal the heads as souvenirs. It is one of a collection of stories told in *The Local Historian's Table Book of 1842* (Richardson), and repeated countless times when news in local magazines or newspapers is running low. This account is very carefully considered, written as an investigative piece entitled *Murder of Margaret Crozier*, by Robert White.

It is preceded by:

'Tis a tale,
Solemn and sad, revealing much of ill,
And vengeance too, without a single trait
Of all-redeeming mercy.

The writer is recording events of fifty years ago. The time lapse causes him to reflect on how time changes truth into tradition.

WINTER'S GIBBET

In 1791 an old lady, Margaret Crozier, lived in part of an ancient defensive tower at The Raw (the row), where she sold drapery and other goods. On 29 August she was visited by two local women who came for a chat before bedtime. They reminded her to bolt her door, but she was unafraid and said she would not bother. On the next day Barbara Drummond came to buy something, saw some thread lying outside the door, and didn't go in. She told one of Mary's visitors of the previous night and a local farmer, and together they went to see what had happened. The door was shut, but unbolted. They found Margaret in bed with a shallow cut to her throat and a handkerchief tied tightly round it. Her palm had been severely cut, and a bloodstained knife was found amongst the bed clothes. She had struggled with her murderer. The door had been forced open with the point of a plough coulter, and there were signs of robbery of muslins, clothing, printed cottons and handkerchiefs. Local people were unaccustomed to crime of this nature, and people came from far and wide to view the site of the murder as people today flock to similar scenes of death (why?). The hunt for the murderer was on.

The scene of the crime was studied thoroughly, and lists of what might have been stolen were made. A reward of five pounds was offered for the conviction of an offender or offenders.

It came to light that two boys had seen a man and two women the day before, 'of a suspicious appearance', near a sheep fold. They had an ass with them, and were eating fat mutton and bread. One boy noticed the gully knife that the man used to cut the meat. 'Being seated on the grass, the man afterwards sang a song illustrative of the happiness of a shepherd boy.' The boy noticed the distinctive pattern of nails on the soles of his boots. One of the boys, Robert Hindmarsh, was later to identify the knife as the one that killed Mary, and the pattern of the nails fitted those imprinted near the house. Others remembered the three travellers, and they had been seen with a loaded ass near to Harlow Hill (on the line of the Roman Wall, further south). The man was six feet tall, strongly made, dark, with long black hair tied behind 'in a club'. He wore a light-coloured coat, light-blue breeches and grey stockings. The women with him were tall and stout, dressed in grey cloaks and black bonnets.

The two local constables set off on horseback towards Tyneside. They passed Harlow Hill and at Whittle Dean they recognised the man they were looking for wandering among some bushes. Some workmen who were building a stone wall nearby were alerted should the police need help, but the man did not resist arrest. They arrested one of the women two miles west of Ovingham. At first the man and woman denied knowledge of each other, but were contradicted when the woman's dog fawned on the man. They were members of Faw Gangs – gypsies. The man was Thomas Winter, whose father and brother had been executed the year before at Morpeth for robbery. He himself was a known thief.

The prisoners were taken to Netherwitton, then to Mitford, where Winter was stripped and his shirt found to have blood on it, to which he attributed to being in a fight. The prisoners were then put into Morpeth gaol. The other woman was found in Tynedale with her mother. They too went to gaol.

As assizes were held only once a year, they were kept in gaol from September 1791 to August 1792, leaving plenty of time for a case to be made against them. The trial was held in the Moot Hall, Newcastle, and lasted for nearly sixteen hours. 'The place was crowded almost to suffocation.'

One of the women with Winter, Jane Clark, alias Douglas, alias Gregg, had what we call 'cased the joint', and had advised the others to rob the house. The other woman was Eleanor Clark, alias Douglas.

Robert Hindmarsh's evidence was crucial, but subsequently put the boy in danger from revenge attacks. He was taken into Mr Trevelyan's service at Netherwitton for several years, was later attacked but escaped on horseback, and was sent to live with the Revd. Mr Johnson of Bywell. Even here he was not safe, and was sent to the residence of Colonel Baird, north of Aberdeen. After eighteen months he became ill, returned home to his father at Whiskershield and died a few weeks later in 1803, aged twenty-two.

The evidence pointed to guilt. One of the prisoners had a nightcap and apron that had been made locally for the murdered woman. Although Winter, despite eleven months' solitary confinement, showed nerve and courage, he stated in his confession that the house was first robbed, and the old woman left alive, but he had sent the women back to see whether she was alarming the neighbours, after which they reported to him that they had 'tied her up from her meat' (as a horse is tied by bridle or halter when its owner does not want it to eat).

The three were sentenced to death. A gallows was erected on 10 August at Westgate. Winter acknowledged guilt, but the women protested their innocence. They were all hanged, the women's bodies going to the Surgeon's Hall for dissection, where one was found to be a virgin.

Thomas Winter's body 'was gibbeted at Sting (Stang) Cross' within sight of The Raw, in the clothes in which he had been executed. His face was covered. 'Bands or straps of iron bound the limbs, also the chest; and there, at the top of the head, were connected with a swivel which was fastened to the arm or short beam projecting from the higher part of the upright shaft forming the gibbet. The shaft itself would be about thirty feet high; it was of an octagonal shape, and the lower part of it was driven full of large headed spike nails. Great difficulty was encountered in hoisting the body, and for this purpose a set of shear legs had to be obtained from Carrick Colliery. Though a very disagreeable spectacle, it was visited by thousands; and when the body began to decay, the smell was so offensive that the horses which travelled the road could scarcely be urged to

158 Winter's Gibbet.

pass the place. The clothes, by degrees, rotted away, and when the bones were loosening from each other, they were hung up in a new sack, tarred inside and out to resist the action of the weather.' As the bones dropped off, the local shepherds buried them. It was reported that someone from Newcastle got the skull.

Later a wooden figure was hung in the body's place, and when this decayed it was replaced by a wooden head. A further replacement of many is what we see there today. Mr White found the treatment of the body very harsh, and felt that it ought to have gone for dissection. He adds that Northumberland at that time was troubled by these Faw Gangs, and that harsh measures were needed to restrain them.

HAUGHTON CASTLE

Where events of violence and mystery have taken place is fertile ground for ghost stories, but sometimes the tale encapsulates some of the fairly common occurrences on the turbulent Border. One such story begins at least in part with passion stronger than political discretion.

Lord Dacre was Warden of the Marches during the reign of Henry VIII. As such he was expected to be just in his dealings with all sides in disputes and not to show fear or favour. Lee (1870) tells how he was suspected of being in league with some of the Reivers, particularly the Armstrongs. Local people tumbled to the fact that Dacre had fallen for the beautiful Nelly Armstrong; he gave indulgence to her kinsmen in return for her favours. A list of grievances was prepared against him to present to the king through Cardinal Wolsey when he paid a visit to York (where he was archbishop). The day before Wolsey arrived, Sir Thomas Swinburne of Haughton Castle and his retainers chased a gang of moss-troopers as they drove stolen cattle towards Scotland, and took prisoners – including the chief of the Armstrongs, who was Nelly's brother.

Sir Thomas put him in his underground dungeon at Humshaugh the day before he and his men set off for York. In two days they arrived in York. Thomas later realised that he had left no instructions for the care of his prisoner. By then four days had elapsed. He did not meet the cardinal, but rode full speed back home. His horse dropped dead at Durham, so he borrowed another. Arriving at his castle, he shouted after his prisoner, but his staff knew nothing. Horrified, he realised that he still had the dungeon key tied to his belt. William Lee tells what happened next:

> The dungeon was opened, and a blazing torch revealed a horror which the very worst fears of Sir Thomas had failed to contemplate as possible. The unhappy prisoner was found lying upon the steps descending from the floor of the vault – starved to death! In the agonies of hunger he had gnawed the flesh of one of his arms!

159 Haughton Castle.

This event then led to the story of the haunting of that castle.

Mary Crozier had been an innocent victim of robbery and murder. In the *Hexham Courant* in 1932, R.N. Appleby Miller retold an equally disturbing story, since set to music, of the murder of 'Joseph Hedley the Hermit', better known as Joe the Quilter.

JOE THE QUILTER

The lane running out of Warden village north is Homer's Lane, a lane in a hollow. Joe Hedley lived there in a simple two-roomed thatched cottage, overgrown with weeds and lichens. It was sometimes known as the hermitage because it was so far away from other houses.

By trade a tailor, he turned to quilting as an art form, so successfully that his work reached Ireland, Scotland and even America. He was honest, independent and hard-working, and welcomed callers. It seems, though, that he was well known to all travellers, and allowed his house to harbour smuggled goods. He had a good memory for stories, and would entertain people who came to buy his skill with all kinds of tales that he had heard. They listened and were encouraged to linger and buy the fruit that he grew in a patch next to the house.

Joe had been married, but this wife had died a few years before his own death after a lengthy illness, which had taken his time and money in looking after her. In the winter of 1823 his house was cut off by snow, and his neighbours were in the same plight, so did not visit him. He was saved on that occasion by the Revd Robert Clark, 'lecturer' of Hexham Abbey, who got through the drifts and took food and other items for him. At that time Joe was between seventy and eighty years old.

Somehow it was rumoured that Joe was a wealthy man, something that happens to a recluse who shrouds his life in mystery. He may have had money, but not since his wife's illness.

On Tuesday 2 January 1826, he called at Walwick Grange for milk and other things, but was never seen there again. The following Saturday he was found dead by one of the Walwick servants, who first saw bloodstains on and around the front door.

Mr Miller graphically describes the scene inside:

> The floor of the living room was littered with things turned out of drawers, cupboards, boxes and every here and there great splashes of now dried and cracked blood, many of them holding in their coagulated embrace masses of grey hair among broken furniture and clock, crockery and fire irons.

Joe's savaged, twisted body was thrown halfway across the door to the other room. His throat had been cut from ear to ear with a very blunt instrument.

The hue and cry was raised, but the murderer was not caught. In the inquest it was established that one of Joe's relations had called on that day at 6 p.m. and sat with him for a few minutes as Joe cooked potatoes for his supper by the fire. The same man the next day noticed Joe's clogs lying on the opposite side of the road, where they remained in the evening. The same thing happened the next day, but it never dawned on him to call in on the old man.

Joe had also been seen on the night of his death at 7 p.m. by a Mrs Biggs, a pedlar from Stamfordham. As Mr Smith of Haughton Castle had passed by at 8 p.m. on his way home from Warden, when all was quiet and still, the time of death was thought to be between 7 and 8 p.m. The knife was not found. Despite a subscription of £150 raised as a reward for information leading to a conviction, no one was convicted, though some were arrested and questioned. Later it was thought that two 'bad-looking fellows' had been seen lurking near the cottage.

The price of Joe's life? Two silver tablespoons, four teaspoons and two old salt cellars of silver network. He was buried next to his wife in Warden churchyard.

The thought of the service of burial for Joe at Warden church casts the final shadow. Perhaps included in that service were words that we may think appropriate to the ending of all life, whether people think of death as the end or a new beginning:

160 Holy Island. *Keith Young*

Oh Lord, guard us all day long in this troublesome life, till the shadows lengthen, the evening comes, the busy world is hushed, the fever of life is over and our work done. Then Lord, in your mercy, grant us a safe lodging, holy rest and peace at the last.

Amid all the beauty of Northumberland, its interest and opportunity, there is always that undercurrent of violence and strife to measure against good things which have made many people happy. No matter how imperfect our knowledge of the past might be, it helps us to see how we arrived and what we value most. We are what we are because the past has made us so.

nine

Optimism

An exploration of Northumberland can stir up curiosity, impress with beauty
and wonder, and recreate in us a new way of seeing the past. Responses can
be oral – putting into words our feelings about places and digging into ourselves
to follow up the responses to what the eye has seen and the senses have felt. We
have witnessed this at work in drama; through creation we become more intense.
We develop a sense of the past as it affects us in the present.

In the summer of 2004 ten young students from Greenfield Community
School in Newton Aycliffe, County Durham, were given a chance through
a Lottery grant to explore what they felt as a result of coming into contact
with prehistoric rock art in Northumberland. Here was a thoroughly recorded
phenomenon of geometric images picked out on outcrop rocks, earthfast stones,
portables, standing stones and on some slabs and cobbles incorporated into
graves. We know much about where they are placed in the landscape, know that
they had a use for over a thousand years and that they were of great importance
to the people who put them there. Yet we do not know precisely what they
meant to people four or five thousand years ago or in what ways they were used
or how their meanings may have changed. The designs link with others not
only all over Britain, but internationally. The symbols of cups and grooves were
manipulated in an individual way so the motifs on the rocks vary in a fascinating
way. It is as though all people inherently find circular motifs satisfying.

The project included the involvement of an artist in glass, a cultural
geographer, teachers from the school and me. A residential long weekend was
planned in north Northumberland, where my role was to take them to some
of the best rock art in Britain. Neither teenagers nor staff had seen any of this
rock art before, and I told them nothing about it beforehand. The object was
to take the group to places where the art is found, to see it in a wide landscape
setting, then to examine it more closely. Too often teaching is knowledge and
worksheet-based, with little room for individual response. Too often we tell
people what to look for and even what they should be feeling about it.

161 One response to the past in a recent exhibition of Greenfield Community School's work.

The first place was the largest panel in England: Roughting Linn. All knew that they were going to see this thing called 'rock art', but we began with a small waterfall in a narrow valley. This place is magical to most, as I have seen with many to whom I have introduced it, and this was no exception.

From there, via a series of deep ditches and walls of a prehistoric enclosure, we encountered the great rock, bathed in sunlight, with every design showing clearly. We were lucky with the lighting. (Colour 26)

If you want people to make their own responses to a site, it is best not to give a talk about it. My approach is to ask what people can see, then pick up observations and questions to give information. It is important to allow people to react in their own way, for they all get something different from the experience.

The second day was spent on Chatton Park Hill, with brilliant views of a great swathe of landscape from the scarp, across the Till Valley to the Cheviot Hills. Here the marked rocks were moulded into the landscape, rich in a variety of imagery. At Ketley Crag the 'wow' factor came into its own, for the superbly decorated rock shelter floor is a work of art in any age, and it has superb views. Again, there was time to take stock, to absorb the place and its implications.

That day ended on the beach at Bamburgh – a change from other landscapes, and, although there was nothing said, everyone began to create their own images, partly a result of what they had seen and experienced, in the sand. Some even created a cist burial decorated all around. A huge spiral was dragged into the sand, motifs with radiates blossomed.

These initial experiences eventually became a dynamic art exhibition called 'Written in Stone' at the Museum of Antiquities, Newcastle, in October, in which work in so many disciplines was combined, for the young people had worked in glass, studied the landscapes in and around their town and worked for a short while with archaeologists at Bamburgh to see how the past was constructed from that evidence.

What emerged from their work was that from a common stimulus of visits and exposure to knowledge of the past, each one had responded differently. That is how it should be if we allow an honest response. For them the past was brought to life through their own minds and senses, and transformed through their experience and selection to a unique offering.

Among the caged prehistoric and other artefacts, gathered together by generations of seekers after the past, amid the superb fragments of Anglo-Saxon sculpture and more, the new creations brought colour and new life to a building that records the past. If we are really looking for the relevance of the past to our lives, seeking some shared visions and experiences with people now long dead and using this as springboard for personal exploration, this exhibition showed what could be done.

And that is a very warming thought on which to end this book.

Bibliography

Atkinson, F. 1977. *Life and Tradition in Northumberland and Durham*. (J. M. Dent)

Atkinson, F. 1980. *North East England. People at Work*. (Moorland Publicity)

Barr, N. 2001. *Flodden, 1513*. (Tempus, Stroud)

Beckensall, S. 1977. *Northumberland Field Names*. (Frank Graham, Newcastle)

Beckensall, S 1995. *Shepherds, Rogues and Angels*. (Abbey Press)

Beckensall, S. 2001. *Prehistoric Rock Art of Northumberland*. (Tempus, Stroud)

Beckensall, S. 2002. *Northumberland: The Power of Place*. (Tempus, Stroud)

Beckensall, S. 2003. *Prehistoric Northumberland*. (Tempus, Stroud)

Beckensall, S. 2004. *Northumberland Place-Names*. (Butler Publishing, Thropton, Morpeth)

Binskey, P. 1996. *Medieval Death*. (British Museum Press)

Charlton, B. 1987. *Upper North Tynedale*.

Corfe, T. 2004. *Riot*. (Hexham Community Partnership)

Dickinson, G. 2000. *Corbridge: The Last Two Thousand Years*. (The Spredden Press, London)

Feaver, W. 1975. *The Art of John Martin*. (Oxford Clarendon Press).

Fletcher, R. 2002. *Bloodfeud*. (Penguin)

Flinn M.W. 1965. Chadwick E. *Report on the Sanitary Condition of the Labouring population of Gt. Britain. 1842*. (Edinburgh University Press)

Frodsham, P. 2004. *Archaeology in the Northumberland National Park*. (CBA, York)

Hadley, D.M. 2001. *Death in Medieval England*. (Tempus, Stroud)

Hartley, S. 1999. *In the Bewick Vein*. (Honeycrook Press)

Hawkes, J. 1996 *The Golden Age of Northumbria*. (Sandhill Press Ltd, Warkworth)

Hoole, K. (Ed.) 1967. *Thomlinson's North East Railway Book*. (David & Charles)

Hoole, K. 1979. *The North East Railway Book*. (David & Charles)

Hunt, C.J. 1970. *The Lead Miners of the North Pennines*. (Manchester University Press)

Jennings D. 1998. *Two (1872 and 1935) Contemporary Accounts of Poor Housing in Hexham*. (Hexham Historian, No. 8)

Jennings D. 2002. *The 1853 Cholera Outbreak in Hexham*. (Hexham Historian No. 12)

Jermy, R.C. *Lindisfarne's Limestone Past: Quarries, Tramways and Kilns*. (Northumberland Library)

Johnson, G.A.L. 1997. *Geology of Hadrian's Wall*. (The Geologists' Association Guide No.59)

Kristenssen, H. 1999. *Memories of Hexhamshire*. (Wagtail Press)

Lee, W. 1870. *Historical Notes of Haydon Bridge and District*. (Hexham Herald Office)

Lees, H. 2000. *English Churchyard Memorials*. (Tempus, Stroud)

Lomas, R. 1996. *County of Conflict: Northumberland from Conquest to Civil War.* (Tuckwell Press)

Longmate N. 1996. *King Cholera.* (Hamish Hamilton)

McCord, N. 1991. *North East History from the Air.* (Phillimore and Co. Ltd Sussex)

Myers, M. and Forsythe, R. 1999. *R.W.H. Auden Pennine Poet.* (North Pennines Heritage Trust)

Neville, H.M. 1909. *A Corner of the North.* (Andrew Reid, Newcastle)

Ormrod, M. and Lindley, P. 1996. *The Black Death in England.* (Paul Watkins)

Under the Public Health Act (11 and 12 Vict.), the following reports by Robert Rawlinson were published by Eyre and Spottiswoode for HMSO, and are dated in order of appearance. They are entitled Report to the General Board of Health on a preliminary Inquiry into the sewage, drainage, and supply of water, and the sanitary conditions of the inhabitants of the town and townships of: 1849 Morpeth and Bedlington, 1850 Alnwick and Canongate, 1850 Berwick on Tweed, 1848, Hexham, 1853.

Pevsner, N. 1992. *The Buildings of England: Northumberland.* (Penguin)

Raistrick A. and Jennings, B. 1989. *A History of Lead Mining in the Pennines.* (Davis Books)

Richardson. 1842. *The Local Historian's Table Book.*

Roberts, I. and West, M. 1998. *Bellingham, North Tynedale and Redesdale.* (Chalford, Stroud)

Rossiter, A. 1996. *The Government of Hexham in the 17th Century* (Hexham Historian, No. 6)

Rossiter, A. (Ed.) 1994 *Cockshaw.* (The Hexham Historian. No. 4)

Ryder, P. 1996. *Bastle Houses in the North Pennines.* (N. Pennines Heritage Trust)

Taylor, N. 2000. *The People's History. Ellington and Cresswell.* (Seaham)

Tuck, A. and Goodman, A. (Eds) *War and Border Societies in the Middle Ages.* (Routledge)

Wells, J.A. 1988. *The Railways of Northumberland and Newcastle upon Tyne.* (Powdene Publicity)

White, N. 1859. *Northumberland and the Borders.* (Chapman and Hall, London)

Ziegler, P. 1969. *The Black Death.* (Penguin)

Index

Numbers in brackets refer to illustrations. Numbers in bold refer to colour plates.

INDEX OF TOPICS

If you are interested in purchasing other books published by Tempus,
or in case you have difficulty finding any Tempus books in your local bookshop,
you can also place orders directly through our website

www.tempus-publishing.com